THE

FORGOTTEN CHILD

Cities for the Well-Being of Children

Henry L. Lennard
Suzanne H. Crowhurst Lennard

A Gondolier Press Book
International Making Cities Livable Council

ISBN: 0-935824-09-X
Library of Congress Card Number: 00-111302

A Gondolier Press Book
Published by
International Making Cities Livable Council
P.O. Box 7586, Carmel, California 93921 USA

Contents

A Personal Foreword

The question that intrigues us is: how do children become fully human, caring and responsible adults, committed to the welfare of others, whether familiars or strangers; how do some children grow up capable of experiencing beauty, joy and laughter, and other children become adults capable of aggression and brutality, without joy or interest in their fellow human beings.

The question then arises: what are the circumstances, the kinds of social, familial, and physical environments that produce one or the other human being, attentive to others or disinterested, emotionally sensitive or anaesthetized.

For years one of us studied the influence of the family environment on social and emotional development. Together we began to think about the role of the urban environment in facilitating or damaging the development of the child.

Since so many children grow up in city environments, or on the city's periphery it has become more and more important to focus attention on features of the built environment, the configuration of places and streets, the character and uses of buildings, their aesthetic quality, how buildings and places relate to each other, whether in a meaningful way, forming ensembles or visualizable patterns, or in a chaotic and indecipherable way.

Especially, we have thought about what messages and values are embodied in the urban environment. Finally we turned our attention to those largely responsible for the meaningless shape of many cities, the architects, planners and developers, and those whom they serve.

Great writers and a few philosophers have taken up the theme of children in the city. But children are not discussed in works about cities by architects, planners, or almost all urban scholars.

Few serious thinkers have done justice to the complexities of the theme, or have examined how cities impact and change the lives of children for better or worse, and they have been "outsiders" to the planning and building professions. Among these, we need to mention Jane Jacobs, known for her community engagement in saving New York's West Village (but trained as an economist); the German psychoanalyst Alexander Mitscherlich, who wrote a provocative and influential small book "The Inhospitality of Cities"; and the British educator Colin Ward.

At a time when children are on the lips of political leaders, cities in North America and Europe are becoming less and less hospitable to children, more exclusively the domain of adults, more difficult to comprehend and to negotiate.

We came to the conclusion that the creation of optimal contexts for the human social and emotional development of the child has little priority for urban leaders and professionals.

Of course, family dynamics, socio-economic position and cultural priorities also influence the process and outcome of socializing and humanizing children and are factors in creating decent or destructive human beings.

But we thought it was time for a different focus, a shift to another paradigm – we consider it a paradigmatic shift from the individual to the social and physical environment, to the places, the buildings and spaces in which children grow up. We propose that children should be considered not only within the context of their family and neighborhood, but also within the context of the whole built environment that surrounds them, its character, beauty or ugliness, its stimulation or dullness, its meaningful or meaningless organization. It is the attributes of this urban environment, the values it embodies, the messages it transmits to the growing child that concern us in this book.

The example of Venice initially was very important for our understanding of this issue. Our experience and observation of daily life in Venice, on Venetian campi (fifteen or more large public spaces) opened our eyes to the intricate relationship between the physical urban environment and social life. We were in Venice almost every year since the early 1970's, sometimes for several months, and spent a great deal of time observing everyday life on the Venetian campo, the activities of children, their encounters with each other, with family members and other adults.

We observed the attraction everyday life holds for the children of the campo; how they relate to each other, the variety and inventiveness of their games, their easy contact with familiar adults and strangers; and we observed the many ways adults show their interest in children not only their own, and in young people. It is on the campo that we can observe most clearly the intricate relationship between the physical environment and aspects of everyday social life, especially with respect to the socialization of children.

It was at that time, too, that we again came upon Lewis Mumford's magnificent book **The City in History,** where he contends that the lessons of Venice have <u>still not been learned</u>.

Through the circumstance of topography, the unique history of Venice whose founders built a city on islands in a lagoon and then connected them with 140 bridges, a spatial configuration was created resistant to vehicles, suitable for the conduct of daily life, uniquely supportive of the inclusion and socialization of children into their community, allowing them free movement through the city and encouraging autonomy. The physical layout of the campo brings inhabitants together to meet and talk, and focuses their attention on each other.

The situation is in stark contrast to that prevailing in so many cities, where the urban environment hinders, abridges, and displays indifference, if not hostility to the lives of children.

It was in July 1977 that we organized our first Conference in Venice on the subject of **Ethics in Health Care**, primarily around ethical problems generated by new developments in family therapy. Among the friends and colleagues we invited were leaders in family therapy and social philosophy.

Again and again our discussion at the conference was drawn to Venice, and what we could learn from Venice about the interrelation between the physical and social aspects of city environments.

It was therefore no accident that we chose Venice to organize our first **International Making Cities Livable Conference** in 1985 for city leaders, architects, planners, behavioral scientists and others. That conference, as well as subsequent conferences held in Venice started off with a discussion of the lessons of Venice, and dedicated one of the plenary sessions to the topic of the *child in the city.*

With one or two exceptions, every one of the twentysix IMCL Conferences held since then, in Europe and in the United States had at least one session addressing this topic. We believe that this continuing emphasis on children as an important topic for urban professionals concerned with cities was unique, but overdue.

Though it was difficult to obtain paper proposals from architects and planners we persevered. We used a number of mechanisms to generate interest, developing and circulating questionnaires on the good city for children among participants and professionals in different cities, but with less than hoped for response.

In 1994, together with our colleague Andreas Feldtkeller who was a member of the IMCL group from the very beginning and who was one of the few planners committed to creating conditions where families and children could again live in the Old City of Tübingen, we organized a Seminar on **The Good City for Children** in Tübingen.

We continued the effort to bring together colleagues around the theme of children and the city in 1996 with the collaboration of Ravensburg's Mayor Hermann Vogler, and then in 1997 with the collaboration of Charleston's Mayor Joseph P. Riley Jr.

It had become obvious to us over the years that this reformulation of how we think about children and the city involved a unique interdisciplinary approach from a new perspective. To do justice to the complexity of the issues involved we needed to write a book.

The book, however, was delayed as we became aware of new interconnections and relationships. Wisdom, our friend Gregory Bateson used to point out, is to recognize "system interrelationships". Among the many new issues that had to be addressed was the emergent culture of electronic violence made possible and amplified by the new electronic technology. We needed to address how exposure and attraction to violence is very much connected to the abandonment of the shared public world, of real places in cities, and the banishment and isolation of children in their homes, and as a consequence, their increased exposure to the alternate world of "mayhem".

We recently wrote: "If we neglect to offer young people human fellowship in <u>real</u> places, the opportunity to enjoy everyday community social life and to be engaged as full participants in celebration and festivity, then their models for conduct and their sources of fantasy will be drawn from their experience with the world of media, electronic games and cyberspace where they are increasingly exposed to images of destructiveness, the horrible and uncanny.

A great deal needs to be said about the connection between characteristics of our urban environment and the emotional desensitization, anesthesia and fascination with violence and destructiveness of children and youth. This too is a subject of this book.

Each chapter of the book deals with a different set of ideas and can be read independently and in any order. But it will be more useful for the reader to review most of the chapters to discover new "patterns that connect" -- the interrelationships that exist between the physical and social environment of our cities.

Henry L. Lennard
Suzanne H. Crowhurst Lennard
Venice, May 2000

Chapter 1

Introduction

In this book we are concerned with developments that have adversely affected the lives of children. Increasing awareness of these factors may, we hope, reverse their potentially harmful long term effects!

The increasing isolation and segregation of children in our cities and suburbs is of special significance. This has meant a loss of freedom for children to explore their neighborhood and city as they get older, their exclusion from varied contacts with diverse adults in a variety of settings, and their consequent inability to learn from personal experience and observation, so essential to social and emotional development. Instead, children have been inducted into an alternate "life on the screen", initially with television, and now increasingly to life on the computer and with electronic games.

The presence of children so characteristic of traditional cities has considerably diminished. In the center of most cities, children are not visible. One can spend a great deal of time, not only in modern American cities, but also in some historic European cities, without encountering children. They have no place, nor are they welcome in the world of commerce.

Urban design and planning decisions are based on the premise that cities exist primarily for economic purposes. Most city centers have been depleted of diverse activities except for commercial and administrative functions. These areas, often busy only from nine to five, become unsafe wastelands at dusk, unsuitable for the presence of most people, and especially children.

The destruction of the continuous urban fabric through architectural ideologies and planning policies has led to the creation of fragmented and chaotic cities. There are architects who claim that their work mirrors the chaos of modern life, and some even celebrate this fact. In creating the modern city, children were not on the minds of architects, planners, and most city leaders. Children, however, need a coherent and decipherable physical urban environment.

Conceptions and values -- how we view our fellow human beings -- also have consequences for the quality of children's everyday life. Whether human beings are viewed as potentially dangerous, or motivated only by self interest, or seen as trustworthy or even altruistic, influences how people behave towards each other in cities, and what values and models of conduct children are exposed to.

Images of cities as dangerous places, and of ordinary unfamiliar adults as dangerous and to be feared, have a corrosive effect when they form the basis for the design of modern cities or their suburbs.

Of interest, too, are the shifts in perception of children, as evidenced by public discussion, media images and social policies; violence of children towards each other occupies more attention and concern than violence towards children by adults.

Increasingly, public attention is focused on the violent child, as if violent and destructive behavior is inborn and not learned through experience and example. Children as "monsters" are familiar media themes, and recent incidents of violence by children towards each other reinforce such conceptions. At the same time, we concern ourselves too little with violence towards children, and a culture of violence that provide the experiences and models for the child's subsequent behavior.

The decrease in community involvement and civic engagement, crucial to the presence, safety and well-being of children within the public realm, is a related phenomenon. The more fragmented the society the less interest and responsibility do adults take for children and youth not their own -- the more they will "look away", rather than take an active role in the lives of children in their city.

Crucial for the failure of the modern city to provide a suitable habitat for its children has been the inability to comprehend the connection between the physical and social elements of cities, and the inability to treat the physical fabric of the city as inseparable from its social meaning and effect. Beauty, coherence, meaning, and justice are values embodied in the physical as well as the social environment. They are essential requirements for optimal human development but they do not receive priority in planning and thinking about cities.

In many North American cities it is difficult for children to get around by themselves. Children's need for autonomy and mobility were sacrificed to accommodate the car. Traffic planners believed that to move working adults efficiently required wide traffic arteries, impassable and dangerous for children. Children's autonomy, mobility and access to their city's resources have thus been increasingly diminished.

Even where children are confined to the city's periphery or suburbs they have become less visible, discouraged from using the street by their parents' fears of real or imagined dangers from strangers or traffic. They are also seduced into staying at home by the appeal of television, electronic games and the computer.

The segregation of children in the city's periphery and suburbs is often justified by the contact with "nature" that such locations offer. Even this is frequently illusory as green areas are asphalted for development. But most importantly, suburbs and tower blocks at the city's periphery do not offer the qualities and experiences essential for children's social and emotional development.

The homogeneity and monotony of most North American suburbs is matched by the miles of high rise slabs surrounding many European and North American cities, characterized by Yale's eminent architectural critic Vincent Scully as "landscapes of hell". Neither the suburbs, nor tower blocks are suitable environments for children. As the microbiologist Rene Dubos, wrote in "So Human An Animal", "Everyone agrees that our cities must be rebuilt. But while technologies are available for almost any kind of scheme imagined by city planners, architects, and sociologists, who knows, or who tries to discover, how the environments so created will affect human well-being and condition the physical and mental development of children?"

For a period of time high-rise buildings were rejected as inappropriate for families with children. Now, however, some planners have reversed course and again promote high-rise buildings as suitable environments for family living.

Children need to be included in the life of the city, and exposed to the stimulation that urban resources offer. Children who do not experience the stimulating social world of a healthy city will have little affection and loyalty to their own city, or to the idea of the city.

Those who do not value the real city promote the "virtual city", and offer to replace children's direct authentic experiences by making "life on the screen" attractive.

Within their diminished life space, children are seduced into spending more of their time at home watching TV, using the computer, or playing electronic games. Even when parents instruct their children how to behave with others, friends or strangers, children can no longer learn from first hand observation of their parents and other adults.

The removal of children from the city to the periphery or suburbs, or their confinement in inner-city compounds, subjects both suburban children and inner-city children alike to homogenous social environments. In both locations they lack contact with a variety of other people. It is only in a diverse social environment that children can develop the social skills required to engage in a variety of relationships. The presence of a broad spectrum of others within the social world of the child is important for children's social development. It is exactly with respect to this issue that the work of Jane Jacobs is so important. In "The Death and Life of Great American Cities" she describes how adults in well functioning city neighborhoods serve as monitors and models for children, while pursuing their own activities.

The de facto amputation of children from the world of the city has major social consequences. These include: children's failure to develop social skills and competencies; failure to become interested in the built environment that makes up a city; and importantly, a failure to learn – from participation, direct observation and example – how to care about and be responsible for fellow human beings.

The isolation of children and youth from the common adult world, their exclusion from the natural learning environments of social life, work and cultural activities, has serious consequences for their emotional and social development. Drug and alcohol use, aggressive behavior towards each other and towards other community members, are among the adverse outcomes of this exclusion of children and youth from the life of cities.

Everything that concerns the organization and design of cities, their legibility, beauty or ugliness, hospitality or brutality, accessibility or inaccessibility, has impact on all who inhabit them.

Colin Ward reminds us that, "If the claim of children to share the city is admitted, the whole environment has to be designed and shaped with their needs in mind, just as we are beginning to accept that the needs of the disabled should be accepted as a design factor."

In the recent past, city-making decisions favored some groups at the expense of others considered to be of less value to the economic well-being of cities. This bias especially neglected children and youth.

Yet no one group or function of the city can long be neglected without doing irreparable harm to the city organism as a whole, just as no one organ or system can be favored at the expense of another in the human organism. With the exclusion of children from the life of the city not only is their well-being imperiled, but also the functioning and vitality of the city as a whole is diminished.

We believe that to design a city that promotes the well-being of children improves the city's livability for other groups as well.

Chapter 2

Effects of the Built Environment

Children grow up assuming that they are the kind of person that their physical environment tells them they are. They see their environment as a portrait of themselves. This is fine as long as the built environment conveys positive values; but for those growing up in derelict inner cities, ugly urban peripheries, or monotonous suburbs, it becomes extremely difficult for family members, school teachers or community leaders to counteract these subliminal messages and instill a sense of pride and self worth.[i]

A sense of identity is gained from the way in which other people relate to one, from their response to one's own needs or actions. A child's identity develops not only from the way in which people respond to them, but also from the way in which elements of their built environment (bearing messages from those responsible for its construction or maintenance) respond to the child. The philosopher Martin Buber wrote that all we encounter "addresses us".

How can a child develop a sense that he is a good person, loved and respected by others, when he grows up in a housing project designed with the expectation of crime and violence, in a sea of potholed streets that the city does not care to fix, surrounded by vacant lots and abandoned buildings that the owners are waiting to develop. As Kevin Lynch says, "children should be living in places that have a clear social and spatial identity, places they can understand and take pride in."[ii]

Responsive and supportive environments promote social and emotional development and lead to responsible behavior. Unresponsive and inhospitable environments, however, generate low morale and low self esteem, a sense of the world as not trustworthy, and contribute to dysfunctional behavior including violence.

Scale, proportion

Every aspect of a building conveys a human message. A building's facade may relate in scale to the human being, with appropriately sized window and door openings, reinforcing a child's realistic appraisal of the human world; or it's scale may be too small (making adults and children feel as if they are in toyland); or too large, as in many corporate headquarters, or as in Fascist architecture, designed to awe and overwhelm adults and children alike; or it may lack human scale altogether, with windowless, blank walls, or sealed glass facades, in a total negation of human presence.

A building's overall size may be human in scale, permitting a parent at the highest window or balcony to see and call to their child on the street (the maximum height is usually five or six stories); or it may be so vast that from the top floor human beings look like ants, and the building overpowers the individual on the street. In a scene from Graham Greene's "Third Man", shot from the top of the Vienna Prater Ferris wheel (one of the highest in the world), Harry Lime tells his friend who is looking down at the people on the ground "Do you really care what happens to one of those dots below?"

A building's entrance often makes a strong impression on a child; some entrances are welcoming -- wide, light, allowing one to see inside, providing a sheltered space where one can decide whether to enter or not; other entrances are forbidding -- dark, hidden, cramped and closed, and generate apprehension.

Feeling and seeing the city

Children learn about the world through touching it: a wooden staircase is warm to the touch; a concrete floor is cold and hard; steel and glass walls are transformed in sunlight from icy cold to burning hot; water is temperamental, changeable, and always fascinating.

The proliferation of prefabricated buildings, and predilection of modern architects for steel, glass and concrete have produced an urban environment of materials that are predominantly cold, hard, smooth, ungiving, a physical environment that seems to reject touch, that holds itself aloof from human contact.

Color has an immediate appeal and emotional impact, particularly on children, who are often more sensitive to visual impressions. Until the twentieth century color was frequently used to beautify buildings and cities.

As far back as the Minoan culture of Knossos in ancient Crete, palace structures were awash with intense blues, yellows and reds. Gothic cathedrals from Chartres on dazzled the faithful with a joyful explosion of colors that flooded through jewel-like stained glass windows. Burano, a centuries-old island town near Venice "where the rainbow fell to earth" is a kaleidoscope of blue, green, purple, red, yellow and orange houses.

Many cities selected a range of colors appropriate to local earth tones -- one may think of the "burnt Siena" earth tones of Siena, Italy; "red Bologna"; or of the sandy earth tones of the adobe city of Santa Fe, New Mexico.

Only in the twentieth century did architects insist that buildings must be devoid of the emotional appeal of color.

The artist Friedensreich Hundertwasser, launched a counteroffensive in the form of extravagantly colorful buildings with golden domes, brightly tiled columns and grass roofs. Time will tell whether his message will have lasting impact.

Children are very observant and often notice details that adults overlook, such as carvings, murals and decorative facades. They observe that some painted facades portray historic figures or events; that others celebrate the bounty of nature; that some decorative designs are graceful, others grotesque; that some are serious, others playful.

Children react spontaneously to these decorative elements and draw certain conclusions. Their imagination and curiosity are stimulated; they wonder about the people who placed the designs there, and the messages they were presenting.

By eschewing decoration, by insisting that buildings must be blank, unadorned, the "modernist" architects have removed this medium for stimulating the imagination.

A connected urban fabric

For the city to make sense, to represent a meaningful social organization, the majority of buildings need to be connected, and related in character and scale.

The way in which buildings relate to each other in the city provides children with a model for how people relate to each other in the society. This model may be internalized by the child as a "prescription" for how they should relate to others. Buildings that are connected, contiguous, part of an ensemble, emphasize interdependence, communication, and sense of community.

A continuous urban fabric of buildings approximately the same height and scale, though perhaps built at different times and in different styles, represents a society in which cooperation and negotiation have taken place, and can continue to take place.

Continuity in the physical fabric of the city is a very important factor in making the city safe. When buildings alternate with abandoned lots streets become potentially dangerous, especially for children.

The shop-house

Throughout much of the Western world the primary building block of the livable city is the "shop/house" with shop, workshop or restaurant at street level and residential dwelling above. The close proximity of the public and the private realms, of living, working, socializing, are what makes the public realm so hospitable, and the private dwelling so convenient.[iii] This arrangement makes a city that is not only socially healthy, but also ecologically sound, eliminating unnecessary travel.

For children growing up in the city the shop/house often provides an ideal environment. The presence of familiar adults on the street, including shopkeepers and neighbors, provides some monitoring of behavior, and also increases the safety of the street for children.

The form of the shop/house varies slightly from culture to culture, but in many cities the buildings are constructed around inner courtyards. For families with little children these courtyards are useful as safe play areas for toddlers, and can function as shared communal spaces for the families living around the court.

Children growing up within a dense mixed use urban fabric are likely to be within walking distance of school, friends' homes, movie theaters, shops, cafes, library, museums, parks, and other places where they can hang out with friends.

They are also more likely to be within easy access of their parents' place of work; parents' time saved in not having to commute long distances may increase time spent with the family. The close vicinity of workplaces of all kinds, -- offices, workshops, studios, professional and service industries, and even industrial activity, affords the child some familiarity with the adult world of work which helps them to identify where their own interests and talents lie. And when the young person begins to look for weekend jobs or part time employment there are likely to be opportunities close to home.

The importance of recovering mixed use communities of "short distances" has been realized by enlightened city planners and some success has been achieved, especially in smaller cities such as Tübingen, Germany and Portland, Oregon in the U.S.

The fragmented city

When isolated buildings alternate with empty lots, creating a disconnected urban fabric, the message is conveyed that there is no continuity in the social fabric of the city, that there is no relationship and no mutual support to be expected between groups in these free-standing buildings. The fragmented city becomes a meaningless city, a city in which meaningful relationships do not exist.

Abandoned and poorly maintained buildings convey to children that adults do not take responsibility for the physical environment. The role model exhibited to children is one of neglect and irresponsibility; within such a context it is not worth caring about objects and possessions. Landlords and property owners neglecting their responsibility in maintaining a sufficient standard in low-income housing, are creating an ugly urban environment which generates resentment and anger in their young residents.

The importance of beauty

Beauty is important to every child, perhaps especially to disadvantaged children. And yet, in the twentieth century, we have permitted cities to evolve with vast areas that are so ugly that, if we can, we adults flee the city as fast as our cars will take us, leaving the poor, and the children of the poor to bear them as best they may.

Beauty is not a purely subjective matter. "Beauty is in the eye of the beholder" means that it is up to the beholder to appreciate beauty, not that anything can be defined as beautiful. But what are the characteristics of a beautiful city or town; and is it possible that such beauty can have a benign influence on children?

We all know that a rose, or a group of trees, or a horse is beautiful; yet wherein lies this beauty? Gregory Bateson, who pondered this question more deeply than most, drew certain principles -- harmony in diversity, proportion, fit, and evidence of balanced growth. As we see from Gombrich's essay on "The beauty of old towns"[iv] these principles are as applicable to cities as they are to nature.

What does a child see on a street in an old city with buildings dating from the twelfth to the eighteenth century: that the buildings are not too different in overall height, and that, while different in style and detail, each building picks up a theme and gives it an individual interpretation -- whether it is in the design of the bay windows, gables, ornamental doorways, or in the subtle variations in color of plasterwork. A harmoniously built city is like a beautiful symphony.

This "harmony in diversity" tells a child that to be unique and different one does not need to cut oneself off from society, to reject one's neighbors, or one's past; indeed, the mutual respect between buildings enhances the beauty and individuality of each.

In a beautiful city appreciation of the underlying principles -- harmony, proportion, appropriate relationships, continuity and unity -- may be perceived by the child as a prescription for behavior.

So also, in an "ugly" city one may discern underlying principles that govern the built environment, such as uniformity and featurelessness, conflictual relations among buildings, uncontrolled development, and these also may serve as prescriptions for children's behavior.[v]

Environmental and emotional anesthesia

In an ugly, deteriorating environment children learn to "tune out". The environment then has a deadening effect on emotional responsiveness and reactions. This numbness and loss of sensitivity to the physical environment is reinforced when their social environment is also characterized by lack of caring, indifference, and brutality of persons toward one another. Children's ability to identify and show empathy to their fellow human beings is diminished as their humanity is suppressed; they may then feel entitled to act brutally and violently to others.

Priority for aesthetics

Ugliness has become so pervasive, so much a permanent condition of the physical environment of our cities that not only has sensitivity to its presence been suppressed, but we have abdicated the right to judge features of our urban environment on the basis of their ugliness or beauty! As the Viennese sociologist Wolfgang Schultz pointed out, the beauty of the built environment has become a taboo subject.[vi]

Cities aspiring to be "livable" must give priority to aesthetic considerations, and the creation of a meaningful physical environment. The physical and social environment of cities are two aspects of the same reality. Just as it was a mistake to maintain the body-mind dichotomy, so it is a mistake to think that city inhabitants can have a good, conflict-free civic and social life in an ugly and physically inhospitable city.

It is not surprising then, that great natural scientists have given thought to the aesthetics of the urban environment. Ethnologist Konrad Lorenz does not hesitate to claim that one finds "the highest incidence of crime in the ugliest parts of town. The Neuerlaa district of Vienna is both the Police Commissioner's biggest headache and the ugliest thing that was ever built in Austria." He adds his view "That such a thing could have been built is explained among other things by the fact that the architects have grown blind to natural harmonies."[vii]

Rene Dubos warns that "young people raised in a featureless environment are likely to suffer from a kind of deprivation that will cripple them intellectually and emotionally."[viii]

Aesthetic considerations must regain the importance they once had in the history of city making, before the idea of the city as a work of art was abandoned. While the claim has been made that aesthetic considerations are relative, there is much evidence to the contrary. Studies eliciting city residents' aesthetic evaluations of their city environments have yielded considerable consensus.[ix]

Beauty in the urban landscape is immeasurably valuable, since it is a free resource, available to all, at all times; and it is no harder to create than is ugliness!

---

[i] Those for whom this premise is not self evident can find support for it in the work on children by the architect-psychologist Sharon Sutton in her book "Weaving a Tapestry of Resistance" and in the experimental studies of psychologist Norbert Mintz, who shows that subjects who were seen in "ugly" rooms were thought by evaluators to be more "ugly" than when the same subjects were seen in "beautiful" rooms.

[ii] Kevin Lynch, **Growing Up in Cities**, Cambridge, MA, The MIT Press, 1977, p. 58.

[iii] See Andreas Feldtkeller, **Die Zweckentfremdete Stadt**. Frankfurt-New York. Campus Verlag. 1994.

[iv] Ernst Gombrich, *"The Beauty of Old Towns"*, in **Reflections on the History of Art**, Berkeley, California, University of California Press. 1987.

[v] While some will argue that judgments of beauty and ugliness are wholly subjective, we would predict that a majority of persons from Western European countries presented with a list of cities they know would agree at least on the most beautiful and the least beautiful!

[vi] Wolfgang Schultz, *"Criteria for Urban Aesthetics"* in **Making Cities Livable Newsletter,** Vol. 4, No. ½, 1994.

vii   Konrad Lorenz, **On Life and Learning**, New York, St. Martin's Press. 1990. p. 38.

viii   Rene Dubos, **So Human An Animal**, New York, Charles Scribner's Sons, 1968. p. 194.

ix   Wolfgang Schultz, op.cit

Chapter 3

Meaning in the Urban Environment

Dysfunctional cities

During the past few decades, family researchers have studied communication in dysfunctional families. In such families behavior is often unrelated and lacks continuity. One family member introduces an idea or subject, only to find it wholly disregarded by the others. The conversation of family members also exhibits a fragmented quality that has been described as a "word salad". Children raised in such family environments become confused and experience a sense of meaninglessness.

In studies of dysfunctional families words such as "impervious" occur frequently. Lyman Wynne comments that in such families it is not customary to acknowledge or confirm each other. Children are not responded to, but rather ignored. Their initiatives and attempts at independence are discouraged[i].

Remarkably, descriptions of the contemporary urban environment are <u>analogous</u> to descriptions of dysfunctional families: impervious family interaction is echoed by the impenetrability of buildings for children, their hard, unresponsive architecture, barriers to accessibility and mobility, and environmental restrictions and control exercised over children's lives. We can add to the list other failures of dysfunctional cities such as banishment of children to inner city ghettoes or suburban enclaves, or their de facto house arrest by parents' exaggerated fears of other human beings; and finally such increasingly popular policies as curfews, offered by city officials as a creative solution to the problems of juvenile crime.

For too many children and young people, life in many modern cities and towns might well be compared to growing up in a dysfunctional family. Developers and architects construct buildings often irrespective of the character of adjacent buildings or local traditions. The dialogue among buildings, that in traditional cityscapes echoed one another in scale, choice of materials and in building elements, is now one of fragmentation and discontinuity. Buildings and the spaces created between them rarely represent an "ensemble"; they do not relate to each other in such a way as to make a meaningful whole.

Yet, paradoxically some architects celebrate the creation of the shock created by a chaotic urban environment. "The fragmentation and dislocation produced by the scaleless juxtaposition of highways, shopping centers, high rise buildings and small houses is seen as a challenge and as a sign of the vitality of urban culture."[ii]

It is clear to anyone who has not been inducted into the mythology of modernism that the celebration of what Lewis Mumford called "spatialized abstractions in utter isolation", -- isolated, free standing building blocks separated from their surrounding streets, or a tangle of freeways dividing neighborhoods -- cannot conceivably be beneficial to young city inhabitants.

The urban or suburban environment of too many cities and towns represent a form of sensory deprivation for children, with little to engage their curiosity, fantasy or affection. As the distinguished biologist Rene Dubos warned, "Young people raised in a featureless environment are likely to suffer from a kind of deprivation that will cripple them intellectually and emotionally."[iii]

While all city inhabitants are exposed to the organization and appearance of cities and towns, the effect on children is profound! Children must visualize their city in their mind in order to negotiate its streets and places. Their internalized portrait of the modern city has become one of disconnected shapes. It is difficult to develop a sense of meaning in a human or physical landscape that does not make any sense.

The understandable city

For life in the city to be a meaningful experience -- for adults as well as for children -- the city's built environment, it's form and organization must be understandable. It must be possible for children to have a sense of where the city center is, where the city's boundaries are, and to know where they live in relation to these two reference points, and how to get from one location to the other. The city as a whole must have a shape that is understandable; each neighborhood within the city must be identifiable, with its own characteristic physical landscape and landmarks.

For a child to understand the variety of functions and activities that constitute the city civic buildings need to be identifiable by their design and appearance. Libraries, theaters, museums and other civic buildings should reflect their distinctive character and purpose in such a way that they cannot possibly be confused with factory or office buildings.

The modern movement attempted to remove meaning from architecture by abstracting architectural design elements and introducing universally applicable industrial systems. We believe this approach to building design limits children's ability to understand the richness and diversity of activities that constitute the city.

The twentieth century legacy

Architectural fashions during the twentieth century have promoted values inimical to the well-being of children.[iv] The internecine warfare of ideologies among architects, played out in flashy architectural journals, excludes any reference to children.

"Most of all", the eminent architectural historian Vincent Scully explains, modern architects "had to be abstract;

they could not under any circumstances be inflected toward their surroundings by Classical or vernacular details or stylistic references of any kind. Such would have constituted an immoral act. Here was another madness to complement the others. It is still prevalent today among many architects who, baffled by the complexity of reality, still insist that architecture is a purely self-referential game, having to do with formal invention, linked madly enough with linguistics, or literature, but not at all with the city or with human living on any sane terms. Such architects claim to reflect the chaos of modern life and to celebrate it."[v]

We hope that in the twenty-first century architects and urban planners will have the courage and vision to create a meaningful urban environment that accepts children as integral participants in the social world; that encourages playfulness, curiosity and discovery; that emphasizes cooperation and interdependence over isolation and independence; and that respects the best qualities of the cultural heritage of the built environment.

The human dimension

It is the human landscape that enlivens the city and gives it its uniquely personal significance. To walk down the street and be recognized and greeted by familiar figures -- the woman at the newspaper kiosk, the neighbor who regularly walks his dog at a certain time, the pizza maker at the window of his pizza restaurant -- is to move in a meaningful human environment that recalls past experiences and conversations.

Being able to recognize people who frequent the street --
the business colleagues who gather for a drink at the
sidewalk cafe on their way home from work, the two
women who are often seen talking together at a certain
corner -- these familiar figures populate and give
meaning to the public realm.

But what imparts greatest significance to the urban
environment are the conversations and encounters and
special events shared with people one knows, family,
friends and neighbors, that take place in the city's public
realm, and the memories of such events that are attached
to specific locations in the public realm.

The historic dimension

For a city to be meaningful it must be possible to
understand not only where one is located in physical
space, but also its history. Too many cities (not only in
North America) have employed a slash and burn method
of spurring economic development, destroying the
heritage of small buildings dating from varied periods,
and replacing them with large scale modern buildings.
The historic diversity of well preserved older sections of
the city provides children and young people with a
visual tapestry illustrating the city's changing values and
fortunes as it developed.

For the experience of the city to be meaningful there
must be a patina of memories of human exchanges or
encounters. When buildings are demolished the
memories that inhabitants associated with those
buildings fade; no account of those events can convey to

the next generation the reality of the setting that the place itself evokes.

Buildings used frequently by the city's inhabitants, or buildings that represent important social functions can be considered "social landmarks". Even if the buildings that house these functions are not historic monuments it is important not to destroy them because they, also, are meaningful repositories of the life of the city.

When significant buildings are necessarily removed, or when industry and trades upon which the city depended in earlier times become outdated, it is still important for children to understand the activities that helped shape the character of their city. Murals and sculptures can bring a city's history to life, particularly when these art works are accessible for children's play, and when members of the community, including children, participate in creating the work of art.

Legibility, imagability

A city is not meaningful if one cannot visualize or find one's way around in it. To find one's way around in any urban environment requires safety, the lack of obstacles (such as wide highways), and the means of mobility (in the case of children this is the use of their feet, or bicycles, or public transportation)[vi].

For the Italian sociologist Walter Baruzzi, the goal should be that children "hold their city in the palm of their hand" "la cittá in tasca"[vii], or, as we might put it, that they know their city like the back of their hand. But for this to be possible, the city must first be legible.

According to the child psychologist Piaget, children first recognize their environment by a series of landmarks, and the relationships between these points of reference, as Kevin Lynch asserts, must be visualizable.

Children's social and emotional development is enhanced in cities that provide a meaningful physical environment that addresses them, that stimulates their imagination and fantasy, and that provides a legible environment for them to explore and make their own.

---

[i]   The idea of "communication barriers" in families is illustrated in a well known and heart rending letter that the novelist Franz Kafka wrote to his father, pointing to the impossibility of breaching the "wall" between himself and his father.

[ii]   Bernard Tschumi, quoted in Karen Lange, *"Los Angeles as a Multi-Center City"* 16th IMCL Conference, Carmel, 1994.

[iii]   Rene Dubos, **So Human An Animal**, New York, Charles Scribner's Sons, 1968, p.194.

[iv]   From Adolf Loos and le Corbusier's severe message that everything from the past must be rejected, all traditions negated; to the "Brutalist" movement of the sixties that promoted harsh, ribbed concrete, brick walls with raked mortar joints, and rusted steel surfaces that made physical closeness (touching) hazardous; to the superficial "pop" and "plug-in" architecture of the throwaway society; to the "postmodernist" style which self-consciously applied classical motifs in inappropriate situations; to the "deconstructionist" style that, by transforming walls into sloping, sliding planes, conveys the message that nothing can be relied on -- each ideological wave, as Yale's distinguished Architecture Professor, Vincent Scully has pointed out, ignored the city and its inhabitants.

[v]   Vincent Scully, *"The Architecture of Community"*, in Peter Katz, **The New Urbanism,** McGraw-Hill, Inc. 1994. p.223.

[vi]   This issue is explored in more depth in the chapter **Accessibility, Mobility, Autonomy.**

[vii]   Walter Baruzzi, *"La Città in Tasca"*, Paper given at the 1996 IMCL Conference in Venice.

Chapter 4

Public Urban Places

In well designed, multifunctional, visually enclosed, safe and traffic calmed public spaces children and young people are able to participate in a rich and varied social life; the campi of Venice, the piazze of Siena, Padova, or dozens of other Italian cities, the market squares and traffic calmed streets throughout the Netherlands, Germany and Austria offer children the chance to observe how adults relate to each other, and practice in learning how to talk to people of different ages and from different walks of life. In these public spaces it is not unusual to see parents -- men or women -- on shopping or business errands accompanied by their babies or small children, meeting acquaintances with other infants, and stopping to introduce the children to each other, encouraging them to make contact with one another, and teaching them how to address adults.

Children learn by observation and participation. By failing to create safe public spaces within multifunctional areas of the city where all inhabitants, old and young, poor and well to do may come together, children are denied the opportunity to observe and learn from varied models of adult relationships.

Varied activities and uses

The best public spaces for children and young people are multifunctional, large enough and articulated enough to accommodate organized events such as farmers markets, impromptu events such as street performers, and adults and children in everyday social life. The variety of people that one is likely to see on any one day, and the changing cast from day to day make the space fascinating for children, but also very instructive. At a farmers' market not only do children experience a vast array of sights, smells and tastes, they also observe how differently the farmers from the country talk to one another, how informally they chat to their regular customers. The clown teaches the child how to gently tease people and make them laugh. Observing the businessmen meeting on their way home provides a model of serious conversation for the child. The lovers embracing at the cafe teach the child how to express tenderness.

The design of public space

The way in which public spaces are designed, their location and degree of accessibility, condition whether the spaces can be used by children and young persons, and whether they provide a supportive environment for social learning.

Whether city dwellers relate to each other with mutual trust and a sense of community, or with fear and hostility, to a considerable extent is determined by the character of the city's streets and squares.

In some cities urban public spaces are designed to support sociability and constructive social exchange; in others they are designed with the clear expectation of destructive behavior.

Surrounding buildings and building uses

It is important for parents to know that their children will be safe playing in the public space while they go shopping, or talk with their friends. Familiar adults "overseeing" the space on an informal basis ensure this safety; these may be adults who live in surrounding apartments, people who work in adjacent shops, cafes, or businesses, or regular users, persons who perform a service, delivering mail, selling their produce at a farmers' market, or newspapers at a kiosk.

Such people will be present in the public space if a high proportion of surrounding buildings are shop/houses, with shops, workshops, cafes and restaurants that generate social life at street level, and apartments above, to provide what Jane Jacobs called "eyes on the street". Those living in the building witness the comings and goings of strangers and acquaintances, and can monitor children's activities. The knowledge that residents in surrounding buildings may be watching increases parents' sense of security.[i]

For this to be possible, apartment windows must be designed to be openable, with sills at a comfortable height for leaning on, or there must be balconies; the apartments should not be higher than four or five floors because beyond that height personal contact to the public space is not possible.

To generate social life, and increase visibility and safety, building facades at street level must permit a high degree of interaction between inside and outside. Businesses that extend their activities out of doors, weather permitting, are extremely valuable because they bring adults (shopkeepers, waiters, etc.) onto the square where they can all the more easily keep an eye out for the children. As Jane Jacobs observed, "the people of cities who have other jobs and duties can, and on lively diversified sidewalks they do, supervise the incidental play of children and assimilate the children into city society. They do it in the course of carrying on their other pursuits."

Focal points

People are naturally gregarious and like to gather where others are present, but they need anchors, or focal points around which to cluster. These focal points may be used by children as "home base", or as a small private territory that they can make "theirs" for a while.

Freestanding fountains, sculptures, planters, or bollards -- objects that offer a place to sit, to lean, to play, to climb on -- function well as anchors. Water is always appealing, especially to young children: fountains, pools and streams in the public space should be accessible for children. Sculptures can also offer children opportunities for play if they are designed with this use in mind; and while the child is playing, the sculpture may also be informing the child about the city's history and traditions.

Children have the creative capacity to turn all objects into elements in their games, and a good strategy is to design the city to be available for their play, rather than to herd children together into fenced off playgrounds. Paving designs stimulate their imagination and may generate walking and hopping games; planter edges and low walls become places to climb and balance; rails can be used for somersaults; low building ledges, pedestals of columns and lamps can be climbed on. In a city that is friendly to children these functional street elements can be designed to accommodate these playful activities.

"The shape of the local streets, stairs and courtyards is important to children (in every culture)", Kevin Lynch observed. "The paving, the trees, the safety, the suitability for informal play, the corners, doorways, nooks and benches where they can meet their friends, the opportunities that places give them to slip away from the parental eye while still being thought safe and under general supervision."[ii]

Seating

To encourage adults and children to linger in the public space requires both formal and informal seating. Parents and grandparents take small children to a public space where the children can play within sight, while the adults meet friends and talk. Adults want to sit comfortably on seats or benches with backrests, and these should be arranged facing towards the play area (a fountain or sculpture), and arranged to facilitate conversation.

Older children playing more active games also need some adult oversight to ensure their play does not get out of hand. Comfortable seating for adults within view of active play areas provides them with an audience and informal supervision.

For many young people skateboards offer both a means of transportation and a challenge to their skills. Skateboarding, however, can be hazardous unless a little used section of the public place, equipped with steps and ramps, and visible to outdoor cafes or public seating is available to them.

Teens and young people need to be able to "hang out" in public places, to observe how adults relate to one another, and to practice meeting and talking with new acquaintances.

Young people usually prefer to gather in areas unlikely to be "requisitioned" by adults, and where they can be more flexible and impromptu. They like to sit on steps, around fountains, or lean over balconies to watch the crowd; sometimes they select a dramatic location to exhibit creative costumes or elicit a response from adults. They prefer places where they can perch, or lean, or lounge while watching the drama of social life around them unfold. Steps, fountains, balconies and ledges, therefore, should be incorporated in such a way that they support young people.

Enclosure

The social value of a public place derives from its ability to focus attention on the people and activities within the space. This is facilitated by visual enclosure, by "walls" that make it feel more like an outdoor room, creating a sense that one has arrived at one's destination, that one need go no further.

While streets encourage movement, enclosed spaces slow people down. People feel more "at home" in an enclosed space, are more likely to linger, to sit, to watch the social scene, or to converse with friends and strangers.

Parents with children feel more comfortable allowing their child to roam within an enclosed, traffic free space; and toddlers have the opportunity to explore small distances alone, knowing that the parent is still within sight.

To facilitate this sense of enclosure entrances need to be small, or barely noticeable. As Camillo Sitte pointed out in his influential book on "The Art of Designing Cities", the ancient and medieval cities evolved many satisfactory solutions -- concealing entrances beneath arcades, curving or angling the access street, closing a vista with an important building, or by using a cliff or mountain to close the view.

Entrances are often bridged by an archway. Passing beneath a dark arch heightens the experience of crossing the threshold, emphasizing the drama of arrival and departure. This clear boundary is helpful for young children who are instructed to stay within the plaza when they go out to play (and helpful for their parents).

Location and accessibility

To be available to children public places must be safely and easily accessible -- that means, by foot, bicycle or public transportation. This requirement also means that the city needs to be structured as a "city of short distances": for children to get access by foot or bicycle to a good public space means that it must be close to where they are living; even by public transport children cannot be expected to travel great distances.

Case studies: Venice and Ascoli Piceno

Historic cities, especially those based on a medieval plan, grew up around a public space, which was used for a multitude of purposes, for a market, for festivals, and for everyday social life. The physical structure of the city surrounding the public place incorporated a fine textured mix of uses that ensured that the public space was socially active. Today, as one can see in many Italian cities, these places still offer many advantages for socializing and acculturating children and young people.

Campo Santa Margherita, in the Dorsoduro district of Venice, one of Venice's ten major public squares, provides an ideal social and physical environment for children. It is a visually enclosed urban space surrounded by shop/houses, measuring roughly two hundred yards by forty-four yards. Approximately

15,000 people live in the neighborhood and use the campo on a daily basis; they do most of their shopping here, they pass through on their way to work or school; older inhabitants come here to walk and talk; young people and university students come here to meet friends; small children play on the campo. Here the children are not out of sight of the adults, isolated on a playground or game field; they are visible, they can stop their play to address or respond to an adult, or to watch how older people are relating to one another.

In this place adults, youths and children negotiate how the space is to be used: boys playing football learn to pay attention to the presence of a frail, elderly person; teenagers learn to control their passion for earsplitting music late at night; little children quickly learn that if they get into a dispute or a fight an adult will intervene to teach them how to make up. In this setting adults become tolerant of normal childhood exuberance and energy. And children learn how to interact with everyone in the community, whether young or elderly, poor or well to do, physically or mentally handicapped.

On Ascoli Piceno's main square, Piazza del Popolo, the tradition of the passaggiata continues to socialize children and young people. On Saturday evening from 6.00-8.30pm the piazza is filled with people of all ages, the elderly, young couples with babies and little children, older adults and youth. They walk slowly up and down, pausing to greet friends and talk; parents introduce babies to each other, and teach toddlers how to talk to each other and to adults. For young people this ritual is great fun and their energy level is high as they mill up and down, call to one another, cluster in fluid groups and flirt. But the model of social relations demonstrated by the adults, and learned over the years, maintains a certain level of decorum.[iii]

We must not be too proud to learn from such historic examples. The tendency of the modern world has been to emphasize the private realm, and as a result, to underestimate the value of the city's shared public spaces. As these public spaces have become less viable as social gathering spaces, so children and young people have increasingly been banished from them. But the potential value to a community of good public places, particularly their value in socializing and acculturating children and youth, is inestimable; the public realm is a resource that society can no longer afford to squander.

Creating public urban places

Urban history tells us that the primary gathering place for all of the city's inhabitants was in the city center. This is still true for many European cities. But in too many North American cities the few public spaces that do exist are in purely commercial areas, or between office buildings. At lunchtime they are filled only with adults, and they become deserted at night.

The mix of uses necessary to provide a continuous public presence (including a residential population) has been lost. Residents have been dispersed to the suburbs; only the very poor have remained in housing projects and urban ghettoes. Commercial activities have moved to shopping malls or commercial strips on the city's periphery.

Some larger cities in Europe are in a similar position, either as a result of having accepted the concept of single function zoning; or, as in English market towns, because the historic market place is used as a car park. Some European cities are now making concerted efforts to restore a substantial residential population in the city center, which will support efforts to create public places that bring children and adults together.

The historic city of Tübingen, Germany, reactivated an old German law that permitted only residential accommodation above the second floor. They encourage the return of families to the city center by providing a kindergarten, junior school, health and play facilities, and by reducing traffic, so that now, many children are growing up in the old city and using the streets and squares to play, meet friends, and talk to adults.

For North American cities the task is more complex: it entails restoring a mixed income residential population and a mixture of uses, but also carving out new public places to serve these social functions. The omnipresent grid plan makes it difficult to create an enclosed urban space to serve as the city's "heart". Moreover, there are generally few unused sites available where a public place is needed most -- at the city's liveliest and most central location.

A city, therefore, may have to choose to create a place out of a central street block. This may mean that the main shopping street, or the street adjacent to city hall, the public library, or other historic landmark buildings must be selected to serve this social function. In this case, not only must the problem of visual enclosure and traffic reduction be resolved, but also building uses may have to be adjusted to increase a residential population, including children, and the support services they need.

Around the central core of many cities -- in Europe as well as North America -- are former industrial or military areas that could more easily be restructured to create genuine mixed use neighborhoods around public places. By careful reinforcement of existing building uses, and judicious infill development, a highly attractive mixed use neighborhood, combining residential, commercial, and business with workshops and small industry, schools, health and recreation facilities can be shaped around a central public place. A development such as this, close to downtown, has the potential to develop a strong community sense, and to provide a good setting in which to rear children.

Architects in the U.K. are developing "urban villages". A new project on the Thames, Greenwich Millennium Village, to be developed on old industrial lands, planned to accommodate a residential population and mix of uses around pedestrian squares and streets, may be able to support public social life that includes children.

The problem in North American suburbs is difficult. Ideally every population group of between ten and fifteen thousand should have its own unique identity and sense of community, reinforced by an accessible public place at its heart. However, density is so low in most residential suburbs, and street layouts so attuned to car use, that to make a successful public place requires a multi-faceted approach. A central location has to be identified that already draws people to it, and that has the potential to be restructured; this may be an existing commercial street, shopping mall, school, or some combination of these elements. A genuine public place (not a privately owned interior commercial space) has to be created, and surrounded by a core of mixed use shop/houses at a higher density than the suburban context allows, as well as work opportunities for local residents. If this physical framework exists then the social functions essential to the socialization of children into membership can be achieved. Finally, this new neighborhood "heart" must be connected to the surrounding low density residential suburb by bicycle and pedestrian networks and to the city center by light rail or other public transportation.

European suburbs often find it easier to maintain identity and sense of community because they have grown around existing older market towns or villages that have maintained a central place and mix of uses. This is true of many of London's neighborhoods, for example, but London's failure to limit traffic still detracts from their use as social gathering, and social learning contexts.[iv]

Conclusion

Cities must provide protected, traffic-reduced public places at the liveliest heart of the city, and in each neighborhood to create a structured invitation for the town's inhabitants to gather, to get to know each other, and as the location for social events and celebrations. Such public spaces offer the optimal environment for socializing children and young people into community members.

[i] In the Venetian campo, which is used by everyone in the community, there are often certain areas identified with specific games: football, for example, is played in an area that won't disturb the older people's use of the campo. If the game gets out of hand, a shopkeeper, or someone at an upstairs window is bound to call to the children to get less boisterous.

[ii] Kevin Lynch, **Growing Up in Cities**, Cambridge, MA, The MIT Press, 1977, p. 13.

[iii] Unfortunately, Ascoli Piceno, like other Italian cities with magnificent public squares (e.g. Siena) serving a panoply of functions of everyday social life, did not learn from its own history. Much of the city's periphery fails to provide public places that can be shared by children and youth.

[iv] In July 1998 the British Government announced that national transportation planning would henceforth emphasize public transport, bicycle and pedestrian planning, and that efforts would be made to reduce dependence on the automobile. We hope that their efforts will be successful and that, in the process, public spaces throughout British cities will be freed from dominance by the automobile.

Chapter 5

The Public Realm as Teacher

Mission of the city

We agree with Lewis Mumford that the overriding function of the city is the "care and culture of human beings". Sharing in all aspects of city life enables children to become full-fledged community members.

Unique to the city is its shared public realm. The terms "public realm", "public domain", "public life" refer to the numerous everyday contacts, meetings, and encounters of city dwellers with each other; to the informal social gatherings and more organized events such as farmers markets; as well as to significant celebrations and festivals: indeed, to all the social transactions and activities that occur in the city's public places, its streets and squares.

Models of social life

Behavior is learned through observation and participation. The public realm provides examples and models of how persons relate with family and friends, with the young and old, with those of different social backgrounds, of different temperament, and with the physically and mentally disabled.

It is essential for children to see what other people look like and how they act, to be able to observe people engaged in a variety of different activities, at work and at play, and in casual or serious conversation. Children learn about human relationships by observing everyday encounters: how friends relate; how adults talk to strangers; how one expresses tenderness, or shows pleasure in each other's company.

As people gathered for a concert on the square in Bergamo one summer evening, we were struck by the diversity of social life, and how much children could learn just by being present and observing others. To our right was an elderly couple gently helping each other to a comfortable seat, while to our left, teenagers were laughing together. Near the entrance were young men teasing one another, and two young couples with prams, talking animatedly to each others' babies which they held so the babies could look at, and touch each other. In the row in front of us a middle aged couple were tenderly embracing; near the stage were two women engaged in an earnest discussion with a young man in a wheelchair; and two young Bergamese were providing some background information to a foreign couple (i.e.

ourselves), about the diverse people who made up the
audience at the concert.

To become full-fledged members of their community
children must learn to pay attention to, and show interest
in others. They learn to do this by observing adults
showing interest in each other and in them.

As they grow up it is important for young persons to
learn how to relate to the many kinds of human beings
who share the world with them. Learning to relate to the
physically or mentally handicapped, to the infirm, or to
the homeless is an especially difficult task. But a society
cannot be called humane or civilized if large numbers of
persons are ignored because their fellow citizens no
longer know how to make contact.

In the public realm there is much for children to learn
from their parents and others who can show them, for
example, how one acknowledges others   --   the
handicapped, the infirm, the troubled -- and how one
confirms them in their humanity, despite their problems,
or "otherness". For indeed, children may one day find
themselves in a similar situation. Unfortunately, many
adults do not realize that <u>all</u> of their behavior represents
a <u>model</u>, after which children pattern their behavior!

Illustration: the homeless

With regard to the homeless, a fact of life in many
American cities and increasingly in some European
cities, parents are by and large <u>not</u> setting a good
example.

City dwellers are becoming used to the presence of the homeless, and the homeless are becoming more visible in some cities.

The causes of homelessness are varied, from urban redevelopment that eliminated housing for the poor, to lack of employment for unskilled workers, substance abuse, or social policies affecting the mentally disabled. Whatever the cause, children now live in a world where the homeless are visible, especially in large cities.

Our concern is that children learn from the way responsible adults, especially their parents, deal with this new facet of their joint social reality. Most parents in the presence of their children will ignore the homeless, avoid them if possible, and if this is not possible, act towards them as if they were not fully human. Granted, an appropriate response is difficult! There are often so many homeless persons in a city that it becomes impossible to acknowledge, or to offer some assistance to every one.

Yet even intermittent attention would set an example, and provide a model for paying attention to fellow human beings. What children now learn from observing their parents' reactions and behavior is callousness to the discomfort and suffering of others.

Behavior that children witness over and over again serves as a model and will have consequences for how children view and act towards others.

Illustration: Gheel, Belgium

It is important for children to learn that the mentally handicapped are "more human than otherwise", that they are ordinary people, like themselves or their parents, with aspirations and sensitivities like their own, and with the same need to be treated as an equal member of the human race. For children to learn this they must, in the normal course of events, observe their parents demonstrate a humane way of relating to such persons.

In the small town of Gheel, Belgium, the local inhabitants have for centuries related to the mentally impaired in an unusual manner – unusual only when compared to other cities: they are treated as fellow members of their community.

The legend of a desperate, cruelly treated English princess finding solace in the town in the ninth century gave rise to a tradition in which families from far away would bring their mentally disturbed or handicapped members to the church erected in memory of the princess, where it was hoped that they might be healed. Some of those brought to Gheel were subsequently boarded with the town's inhabitants. Centuries of learning to treat the mentally disturbed and handicapped as members of their own family has created a society in which children immediately learn to relate to them as ordinary human beings, despite occasional bizarre or disruptive behavior.

Facilities in the town, such as restaurants, shops, and parks, are shared by the residents of Gheel and the

"patient population". Over and over again children see
how adults relate to their mentally ill and mentally
handicapped fellow townspeople. In our visits to Gheel
we observed that, as a result of their experiences,
children and young people relate naturally, and without
fear or aversion to the mentally handicapped and
mentally ill.

Though the changing economic basis of the town and
modern technological treatment of mental disorder have
led to a decline in the number of "patients" the
inhabitants of Gheel still take pride in its special history
and quite unique social pattern.

There are cultural differences in the degree to which
tolerance is shown towards those different from oneself,
especially those who behave unpredictably and are
troublesome. Italians, as we have observed, are by and
large more likely to be accepting of deviant or bizarre
behavior in public than are Germans.

Differences in the ability to tolerate and relate to those
who exhibit more disruptive behavior may be related to
patterns of family interaction and child rearing. Infants
who receive love and attention from their parents, even
when they are difficult, grow up feeling secure in their
own identity, and will be patient and attentive towards
others.

In cultures that emphasize training and punishment over
"nurturing", children grow up intolerant of deviance in
others.

Children and the world of adults

Children need to experience themselves as part of the social life of their city; they need to be recognized and respected.

So much of what needs to be learned cannot be learned only within the family or school context. Children need to understand how their parents and other adults spend their working days. It is valuable for them to have access to this world of work, to see people engaged in different activities, and to encounter people in different trades and professions. It is important that they have a realistic idea of how their city works, of the varied activities necessary to a well-functioning city, and the broad choice of occupations from which they may choose their future.

Some cities have recognized children's need to observe adults at work. In some Viennese neighborhoods shops, businesses, crafts and trades willing to allow children to come in, to look around and ask questions placed a sign in their window, "Spy". The children learned about the type of work that takes place there, but they also learned how to talk to different people, in different walks of life, from varied backgrounds.

In traditional cities, and still today in some European cities and towns, access to the city's varied trades and professions was easy: children lived in mixed use areas within walking distance of shops and workplaces. For children living in today's sprawling suburbs independent access to the industrial "parks", business districts or commercial centers is virtually impossible. This is an additional argument for rebuilding the city of "short distances", fine grained mixed use neighborhoods based on pedestrian access.

In some U.S. cities "Mentoring" programs are gaining ground: children, particularly those "at risk", are assigned to an adult in the community, with whom they spend some hours each week. They accompany the adult in his or her daily work, meet the people they work with, and talk to their clients and fellow workers. When this works well, the mentors feel that they themselves have benefited from seeing their world through a young person's eyes; and the children feel that they have learned something about the realm of work, and that adults have taken them seriously.

Social learning

As Jane Jacobs tells us, "The people of cities who have other jobs and duties... can, and on lively sidewalks they do, supervise the incidental play of children and assimilate the children into city society. They do it **in the course of carrying on their other pursuits.**"[i]

Many people are required to provide suitable models for the socialization of children. The skills involved in speaking with others, making contact, resolving differences, and taking pleasure in social relationships cannot be acquired only from one's own family, especially from families who are already deficient in their verbal and social repertoire. Much can be learned if children have the opportunity to participate in the social life of their city and observe how adults act in their encounters and relationships.

Seeing and hearing

It is only in the public world that we see, and are seen, hear and are heard by others who view the world from a vantage point different from our own. In public we see and hear people who come to the common world from different vantage points.

What is happening in our cities today is that contact and dialogue occur within groups segregated from each other, where all who engage in this dialogue hold similar views, and speak from similar premises, and where the character of social relations are quite similar, whether in the affluent homogeneous suburbs, or in the social contacts among the residents of an urban public housing project.

To become a fully developed social human being involves the skills to engage in the full spectrum of "authentic" human interaction, i.e. to be attentive, to respond appropriately, to know how to live with the different kinds of human beings with whom we share our neighborhoods and cities. Many persons, especially children and young people lack these social skills and competencies.

Social problems

Major social problems are directly linked to the impoverishment of the public realm: to the absence of good models of relationships, and to the lack of practice and skills in human discourse.

The use of physical violence as a preferred mode for settling differences among young people may be partly explained by a lack of knowledge and competence in utilizing other ways of making one's position known, and achieving the desired ends.

Some drug users attribute involvement with addictive drugs such as heroin to an inability to talk and relate to their peers, or to strangers. Drugs provide young users with a sense of closeness and intimacy; they feel more competent in social relations; it appears that they have achieved experiences that ordinarily come about as a result of repeated participation and practice in social interaction. Yet, the intimacy and sense of being close to others is illusory, and vanishes once the effect of the alcohol or drug has worn off. The substance user who has not been part of a communal world did not learn the skills necessary to establish and maintain reciprocal relationships. Interestingly, of central importance in therapeutic communities are group meetings where members learn the skills of self expression, conversation and dialogue.

Learning distrust

Everyone, including children, parents, teachers and other adults, is exposed to the media and is influenced by how the social world is portrayed on television, in the movies and in magazines.

How children think of adults, and how they relate to them is the result of those models of social life they are exposed to in real life and in the media. Models presented in the media are prone to amplify a particular conception of social reality. If these conceptions are not counteracted by positive experience in intact and vital urban settings dysfunctional values and attitudes will result.

If the media focus on rare but dramatic instances of child abduction or molestation by strangers, but give scant attention to the much more frequent parental abuse and mistreatment of children, mistrust of unfamiliar adults increases among children, and among their parents and teachers who amplify the message. Parents who portray strangers as being likely to attack children increase children's mistrust and magnify their fear of ordinary adults. Children are being taught to mistrust strangers, to treat them as potentially dangerous, and to avoid contact if at all possible.

This atmosphere of distrust can easily be felt by anyone who has engaged children in conversation in the shopping malls of North American cities, or has volunteered assistance to a child in trouble.

Learning to distrust strangers also fosters reliance on family members as the only source of safety and support. Yet, in some instances family members provide poor models for children to learn to become competent and good human beings; and not infrequently, family members subject their children to physical violence, or may unintentionally harm their children through pedagogic theories, or child rearing ideologies.[ii] That any mother or father is, a priori, to be preferred to any other community member whether familiar or stranger, is not a tenable assumption!

Learning trust

Trust is an important feature of human relationships --
the basis for social, emotional and economic transactions
among humans. Instructing young persons to trust
others, and to be trustworthy themselves, establishes an
important trans-generational legacy.

When the public realm has not been diminished ordinary
adults constitute an important resource. The
community's adults become both models and teachers,
and also act as monitors and guardians of children in the
public realm.

Viewing ordinary adults in an unfavorable light
preempts an important social resource -- the
community's adults -- who could otherwise serve as
models, and as monitors and guardians of children in the
public realm.

---

[i]   Jane Jacobs, **The Death and Life of Great American Cities**, New
York, Random House, 1961, p. 81.
[ii]   Alice Miller, **For Your Own Good**, London, Virago Press, 1984.

Chapter 6

Accessibility, Mobility, Autonomy

At every age level children acquire an increased level of autonomy – the ability to take steps on their own, safely, and unaided by parents. The toddler, as soon as he can stand, is encouraged to walk by himself. He may fall, but it is the parents' responsibility to ensure that the place where he falls will be safe, and that he does not hurt himself.

The four year old should be able to explore the immediate neighborhood where she lives, and make small trips on her own to a friend's house down the street. The block on which she lives must be safe for her to negotiate by herself.

The ten year old has a great curiosity about the larger social world of his town or city, and should be able to make longer trips on his own, by foot or bicycle or public

transportation.   Clearly, the extent to which children
have mobility and are not dependent on others to take
them where they wish to go is strongly influenced by the
degree to which their city is accessible by foot, bicycle
and public transportation.

Children have been increasingly excluded from the life of
the city as traffic has made streets dangerous. Fear for
their children's safety prompts many parents to forbid
them free mobility. The unwillingness to reduce speed
limits, the lack of pedestrian routes, bicycle networks and
public transportation send a signal to young people that
their community does not care to make their city
accessible for them, and restricts their autonomy in
moving around their city until they reach driving age.

"Traffic limits the lives of children immeasurably more
than it affects the lives of other people" observed Helmut
Holzapfel, transportation planner from Kassel. "There
are some people who believe that children should not be
permitted certain behaviors in cities: they even say the
child should only be on the street when it has become an
adult. But such a recommendation does not do justice to
the question, how children should live in cities and how
they should grow up with some degree of independence
and autonomy."[i]

While U.S. cities are easily accessible for automobile
drivers, twenty-five percent of the population is under
the driving age.   If children are to be given the
opportunity to develop autonomy, cities and suburbs
need to make strenuous efforts to reduce the volume of

automobile traffic, and to improve public transportation, pedestrian and bicycle facilities.

Vehicular traffic system

Any traffic policy that disrupts the easy flow of pedestrian movement limits a child's opportunity to walk to school, to the playground, to the park, or to visit friends. Very broad traffic arteries are especially dysfunctional because they are almost impossible for children to cross. Over and over again we have watched children in Atlanta, Phoenix, San Jose and other American cities risk their lives trying to cross six and eight lane highways, where the widely dispersed traffic lights -- if they exist at all -- are timed to traffic, not to pedestrian needs.

There are appropriate, and inappropriate ways to permit children to cross major traffic arteries. It is not a good idea to make them use tunnels and bridges; far better is to reduce the speed of traffic, to reduce the number of traffic lanes to be crossed, to provide traffic lights, islands, circles and raised crosswalks.

Traffic quietening

The greatest threat to children is from fast moving traffic. Studies show that children have only a fifty percent survival rate when hit by a vehicle traveling at 30 mph., but a ninety percent survival rate if the vehicle is traveling at 18 mph.[ii]

Paralysis and serious injury are only the tip of the iceberg of the non-lethal consequences of the car. The psychic consequences of automobile violence are often overlooked. When children are victims, there are psychic consequences for them in later life. Even the fear of an accident changes the lives of children dramatically.

Streets must be made safe for children to negotiate on their own. Clearly therefore, it is incumbent on transportation planners to reduce the speed of traffic, a major cause of death and injury to children, especially through residential neighborhoods.

In "The Child and the City" Colin Ward explains how the "assumption that the car driver has a natural right to take his vehicle anywhere in the city has, quite apart from the threat to life, gradually attenuated many of the aspects of the city that made it an exciting and usable environment for children. The street life of the city has been slowly whittled away to make more room for the motorcar. Whole areas that were once at the disposal of the explorer on foot are now dedicated to the motorist. The city, which used to be transparent to its young citizens who could follow the routes across it unerringly, is now opaque and impenetrable. Try to find your way on foot across Glasgow or Birmingham, or across inner London, just to see how impossible it would be for a child. In the American city such a walk has long been unthinkable."[iii]

In Erlangen, Germany, as in many other European cities since the 1970's, speed limits were lowered to 30 kilometers per hour (about 18 mph) throughout the Historic District. "This concept has been initiated in my city and it's wonderful to see how the children come back to the street," said Erlangen's Mayor Dietmar Hahlweg. "This has had enormous advantages for safe bicycle riding and safe walking."[iv]

Like hundreds of other European cities, Erlangen has also introduced "traffic calming" mechanisms through street design features -- widening sidewalks, introducing medians and circles, "necking" the traffic lanes at intersections, and constructing raised and ramped "table crosswalks" at the height of the sidewalk in order to slow traffic and make streets safer for children.

Beginning in the 1980's many streets in residential areas have been turned into "Wohnstrasse" (Living Streets), where parking is available only to residents, through traffic is impossible, and vehicles must travel slowly and give way to pedestrians and playing children. Many "Wohnstrasse" are repaved with stone paving, and planted with trees and climbing plants, and have blossomed as public "parlors" for people to meet, and as locations for outdoor cafes and restaurants, ensuring public presence on the street, and opportunities for a sense of community to develop.[v]

Public transportation system

The study by Wolfgang Rauh of the Verkehrsclub (Automobile Association) of Austria has shown that one streetcar every ten minutes can substitute for a four lane highway filled with traffic. An obvious way of reducing the volume of automobile traffic, while also improving accessibility for young people is to provide high quality public transportation.

In many cities children's social relationships are dependent on their parents, in that the children can only get together if transported by their parents. This severely restricts their ability to develop autonomy. For children and young people to become independent of their parents, therefore, requires a good public transportation system that runs frequently near where they live, that they can take not only to school, but all around the city. The service must also run through the evening, so young people can meet with friends, or go to community events or to the movies and get back home after they conclude. The service must also be safe, pleasant, and comfortable, so that many adults will choose to use it as well, in preference to the car, as the most efficient means of getting around.

Costs of subsidizing public transportation must be weighed against the costs of private transportation and parking, costs of additional congestion and accidents, costs of increased noise and air pollution, etc..[vi]

Land use planning

For public transportation to be a viable alternative to automobile use, or for journeys to be short enough that they can be accomplished by foot or bicycle, requires a moderate density of land use, and a mix of uses that create a "city of short distances". Schools must be close enough to where children are living that walking or bicycling to school is possible; shops, the corner drug store, the ice cream parlor, the coffee shop, the movie house, the public library need to be within easy reach by foot or bicycle.

As Germany's preeminent transportation planner, Hartmut Topp explains, "Freezing the total traffic amount by creating a city-structure of short distances is the overall objective of urban compatible traffic planning. To this aim school, work, shopping and recreational facilities should not be centralized, but decentralized within the city quarters. Nearness, mixed use and varied usages create pedestrian traffic and urbanity."[vii]

A city of short distances is a city of neighborhoods, each with a strong sense of identity and community; with a mix of uses, and mixed income residents. The neighborhoods are densely built with a continuous urban fabric at their center. They are constructed around a pedestrian core that facilitates the development of social life and community, easily accessible by foot or bicycle from all parts of the neighborhood, and by public transportation from other neighborhoods within the city. The urban structure that we are describing here is exactly the kind of urban environment that is not only socially and ecologically sound, but that provides the best, and most stimulating environment for raising children. The lack of stimulation and social contact, so characteristic of suburbia (once touted as the best environment for raising children) in fact, limits children's optimal social development.

Bicycle networks

A good system of bicycle lanes throughout the city permits fast and inexpensive access for young and old. The bicycle lanes must be constructed as an interconnected network, carefully designed to avoid, as much as possible, crossing traffic lanes, and where this is inevitable, providing traffic lights and bicycle crossings that reduce the risk of accidents.

In the suburbs and at the city's periphery, where public transportation is not as frequent, children are particularly dependent on their bicycle.

Some European cities have been very successful in promoting bicycle use. Erlangen created a bicycle network of 175 kilometers (109 miles), much of it independent of the roads, and as a result, twenty-five percent of all inner city journeys are made by bicycle. Some bike lanes are entirely new routes, especially those connecting to suburban districts. Bike lanes have been built along the canal embankments, across fields, and out into the surrounding countryside. Large parking areas for bicycles have been created by removing car parking spaces. Special signposts direct cyclists through the city, and a detailed map produced by the City shows all bike lanes and provides additional information for cyclists.[viii]

Pedestrian networks

The safest streets for children are streets with many familiar adults, and without automobiles, or with traffic reduced in volume and speed. For American cities this goal seems to be elusive. The pedestrian shopping streets familiar to some Americans are purely commercial areas; they are busy during the day, but impersonal, deserted and possibly dangerous at night. These do <u>not</u> provide the appropriate model for child-friendly pedestrian networks.

Streets that function well for pedestrians – especially children, have a fine grained mix of uses, typified by the traditional "shop/house". The shops generate activity at street level, and the apartments above provide a permanent population with "eyes on the street" (to use Jane Jacobs' term). Their jurisdiction over activities in the street, and the sense of community that develops as residents get to know one another help to ensure the street's safety. A variety of contacts among adults on the street offer children opportunities to observe, and learn how to interact with diverse people. Streets like this still exist in European cities, and did exist in North American cities through the nineteenth century; but twentieth century planning concepts required that this mixed use fabric of shop/houses be replaced by single function development – office blocks, commercial strips, and areas of housing, and the streets were redesigned for the primary function of vehicular movement.

In hundreds of European cities spared from twentieth century reconstruction, where, thirty years ago, the automobile reigned supreme, virtually the whole of the inner city has now been turned into a largely traffic free area. This approach, combined with efforts to increase the residential population in the city center, and improved public transportation to outlying residential areas, has been successful in making some city centers, with all of their resources -- museums, theaters, historic heritage of buildings, interesting streets and squares, shops, and the whole adult realm of work -- more accessible to children. The educational value, and stimulation of the child's curiosity cannot be matched in a suburban environment.

To be usable for children the pedestrian network should be like a continuous spider's web throughout the city, beginning at the door of the child's home and extending throughout the city, along pedestrian streets, alleys, wide sidewalks and squares, uninterrupted by dangerous traffic crossings.

Dietrich Garbrecht, author of an influential book "Gehen: ein Plädoyer für das Leben in der Stadt" (Walking: a plea for life in the city) advocates: "We should not think in terms of islands or oases for walking but in terms of networks as we do with respect to car driving. Areas for walking should not be distributed over space as unconnected points, pedestrian precincts, residential streets; instead they should consist of interconnected footways -- the threads -- and foci or nodes -- the knots."[ix]

Where traffic needs to cross this pedestrian network traffic lights should be timed to pedestrians, traffic speed limits should be reduced, and sidewalks should be extended to reduce the number of traffic lanes to be crossed ("necking"). The crosswalk, distinctly different in color and texture from the asphalt vehicular surface, should extend across the traffic lanes at the same height as the sidewalk. The traffic must slow down to negotiate the gentle ramp over the pedestrian way.

The safe city for children

The city must become a safe environment for children and young people. Children must be safe from the danger of being hit by a vehicle. Many measures outlined above, which are already being taken in Europe to reduce traffic speed and limit potential conflicts between vehicles and pedestrians should be introduced in North American cities if we value the lives of our children, and if we want to provide for their optimal social development, that includes some measure of autonomy in their city. [x]

Traffic issues are not the only impediments to making the street safe for children to negotiate by themselves. To make streets safe social environments it is essential to rebuild neighborhood communities with a continuous presence of familiar adults on the street. This was characteristic of traditional cities with a high density and continuous mixed use urban fabric. In most North American cities, as well as in some larger European cities such as Frankfurt, London or Milan, this traditional fabric has been destroyed by giving priority to high density unifunctional development: the high rise skyscrapers that replace the continuous fabric create an overly dense residential or office population in which strangers replace familiars, and sense of community is lost. They also overburden the street with vehicles required for delivery and access.

We can still learn from well maintained traditional cities
that have kept a human scale, that are compact,
accessible and safe for small children, that provide many
public places with little or no traffic, accommodating a
very full urban social life, with many people who know
each other, shopkeepers and inhabitants who monitor
behavior in the space. In this kind of traditional city
there is a rich social environment to monitor behavior,
and the opportunity for children to exercise a great deal
of autonomy.

---

[i]   Helmut Holzapfel, Comments at the Ravensburg Seminar on **The Good
City for Children** May 1996

[ii]   Relationship between speed and risk of death. Study by the VCÖ,
(Verkehrsclub Österreich), Vienna, Austria.

[iii] Colin Ward, **The Child in the City**, London. The Architectural Press,
Ltd.

[iv]   Mayor Dietmar Hahlweg, Mayor of Erlangen, Germany. Talk given at
the **19th International Making Cities Livable Conference** on *Children
and Youth in the City*, Charleston, SC, March 1997.

[v]   See: Chapter 14, "Erlangen" in **Livable Cities Observed. A Source
Book of Images and Ideas for City Officials, Community Leaders,
Architects, Planners and all Others Committed to Making Their Cities
Livable** by Suzanne H. Crowhurst Lennard & Henry L. Lennard.
Gondolier Press, 1995.

[vi]   Study by the VCÖ (Verkehrsclub Österreich) shows that when all costs
are taken into account, public transportation is less expensive than the
automobile.

[vii] Hartmut Topp, *"Philosophy and Mechanisms of Traffic Calming"* in
Making Cities Livable Newsletter, March/December 1991. p.2.

[viii] See: Chapter 14, "Erlangen" in **Livable Cities Observed. A Source
Book of Images and Ideas for City Officials, Community Leaders,
Architects, Planners and all Others Committed to Making Their Cities
Livable** by Suzanne H. Crowhurst Lennard & Henry L. Lennard.
Gondolier Press, 1995.

[ix]   Dietrich Garbrecht, *"Walkability: A Prerequisite for Livable Cities"*, in Ben Farmer & Hentie Louw (Editors), **Companion to Contemporary Architectural Thought**, London & New York, Routledge, 1993.

[x]   A U.S. initiative to promote the **Accessibility Rights of the Child** was announced at the 19th International Making Cities Livable Conference on CHILDREN AND YOUTH IN THE CITY, in Charleston, South Carolina, in March 1997. Among those supporting the movement were Co-Sponsor of the Conference Mayor Joseph P. Riley, Jr. of Charleston, and other mayors in attendance (Mayor Nancy Graham of West Palm Beach, Florida, Mayor Carol Opel of Waukesha, Wisconsin, and Mayor Gary McCaleb of Abilene, Texas). The mayors agreed to open a discussion of the **Accessibility Rights of the Child** at the U.S. Conference of Mayors, and to take this initiative to the National League of Cities.

Mayors, council members, planners, architects and youth coordinators from across the U.S., Canada and Europe had gathered in Charleston to consider how to make cities more livable for children. Mayor Opel, of Waukesha, WI, challenged President Clinton to make evident his concern for the nation's children by maintaining -- or better, increasing -- ISTEA funds for public transportation. Mayor Riley announced that he is putting together a city wide plan for Charleston to slow automobile traffic on neighborhood streets and some main streets. "I am convinced -- and this conference makes me even more convinced -- that we need to reduce the speed of traffic through our residential neighborhoods", Riley said.

Chapter 7

How We See Each Other

Our assumptions about the nature and character of human beings, and how we perceive others, affects how they act towards us. These images and assumptions also have consequences for the quality of city life, and most especially influence the well-being of children.[i]

Whether we think of fellow human beings as potentially dangerous, aggressive, motivated by self-interest, or see them as trustworthy, even altruistic, determines the models of conduct to which children are exposed in cities.

The psychiatrist Leon Eisenberg distinguishes between theories about natural phenomena and views held about our fellow human beings. Eisenberg writes, "The planets will move as they always have whether we adopt an egocentric or heliocentric view of the heavens... but the behavior of man is not independent of theories of human beings. What we choose to believe about the nature of man has social consequences."[ii]

Descriptions of persons then become prescriptions for behavior! Descriptions of others as dangerous or untrustworthy have implications for how we act towards them. Such descriptions become self-fulfilling prophecies. When reflected in planning and architecture the result is an environment that encourages urban dwellers to avoid each other. The media amplify negative images and portray cities as threatening and dangerous places. Even when cities are relatively healthy they are not immune from disruptive effects of such negative images, especially images of unfamiliar persons and strangers. Fear of others has implications for the way cities are designed -- whether or not there are urban public spaces, whether street life is encouraged, and therefore whether city centers are populated or deserted.

Fear of one's fellow citizens, preoccupation with the dangers and unpleasantness of urban life has led millions of Americans to lead lives of self isolation, not only in suburbia but in gated compounds, where access is limited to those who live in the compound. So far the concept of the "gated community" is a particularly American phenomenon and is still rejected by European civic leaders, even though a few European resort developments have begun to take on an analogous character.

The proliferation of segregated housing areas in America's cities and suburbs, often with limited infrastructure and few cultural and social resources, has a damaging effect on children's lives, restricting their autonomy and their ability to participate in diverse forms of urban life. Parents are especially afraid for their children and figuratively or literally keep children on a leash. As families withdraw into suburban communities or are forced into urban ghettos, the life space of children diminishes even further.

According to Sissela Bok's review of the relevant literature[iii], children themselves were made afraid by the continual media coverage of a single case of abduction and killing. Sissela Bok points out a related dysfunctional result of keeping children at home because of this fear of strangers: their resultant exposure to TV and video games with violent content which further reinforces their fear of strangers and the public realm!

An illustration: Monterey, California

In Monterey, California, a small city that ranks very low in incidence of crime, especially violent crime, many parents are now picking up their children from school, even when children live quite close and could easily walk home from school by themselves.

There had recently been national media attention to one incident of the abduction and murder of a child some 150 miles north of Monterey. Of course, the protection of every child is important, but we would be more convinced of the seriousness of society's, and parents' concern with children's safety if it was also exhibited in relation to the thousands of children who are killed and maimed by cars on the streets and highways of California, and the country.

Real estate developers base their design of suburban developments on assumptions about the alleged dangers of city life, and in part may amplify the fear of the city as a promotional strategy. In creating gated settlements they contribute to the distancing and segregation of people from each other.

It is ironic that, while the fear of strangers has increased during the last twenty years, family members (parents, and relatives) are themselves often dangerous to children, and becoming more so. Documented cases of child mistreatment in the United States over the past seven years have increased from over one million three hundred thousand, to over two million nine hundred thousand cases. They also found that "the number of children who were seriously injured nearly quadrupled over the same time period from about 143,000 to more than 572,000." And the majority of those involve mistreatment of children by their own parents and relatives.[iv]

Even if some of this reported increase in child mistreatment is in part due to greater awareness of the problem it raises serious questions about the prevailing view that the greater danger to the child is from adult strangers.

Despite the fact that children are most at risk from their own family members, the pervasive fear is of strangers and less familiar adults. Children are discouraged from contact and warned against conversation with persons they do not know. The prevalence of such distrust of unfamiliar adults limits the monitoring and educative role that other adults assumed in functioning communities, and still do in cities with an active street life, and populated urban places.

As Jane Jacobs pointed out, "Planners do not seem to realize how high a ratio of adults is needed to rear children at incidental play... only people rear children and assimilate them into civilized society."[v]

"It is a folly to build cities in a way that wastes this normal, casual manpower for child rearing and either leaves this essential job undone -- with terrible consequences -- or makes it necessary to hire substitutes. The myth that playgrounds and grass and hired guards or supervisors are innately wholesome for children and that city streets filled with ordinary people, are innately evil for children, boils down to a deep contempt for ordinary people."[vi]

Role of familiar adults

Jane Jacobs provides us with many examples of how adults fulfill this role in intact, well functioning urban neighborhoods. If children are made afraid of every adult, they cannot turn to adults for help if in trouble; and if adults are intimidated from making contact with children by the prevailing ethos, they cannot advise, or intervene when children seem to need help. Jane Jacobs particularly emphasizes the role of shopkeepers who know the neighborhood children.

We suggest that concern with dangers to children from adults is diminished whenever there is a great deal of contact among a city's inhabitants; where there are lively public places; where children share the social world with adults during the course of the day, and during special social events. In such circumstances children and adults are known to each other, and familiar adults become a resource for the socialization and protection of children.

There is ample evidence to suggest that the greater the sense of community, the more activities and events shared by city dwellers, young and old, poor and well-to-do, the more difficult it becomes to maintain distrust of one's fellow citizens![vii]

Cities where there is less distrust

It is obvious to visitors to many Western European cities and towns that the level of fear and distrust of unfamiliar adults is by and large lower than in most American cities.

It would be difficult to frighten the Sienese or Venetians into abandoning the pleasures of their numerous public community events that involve all segments of the population. Nor would the inhabitants of Munich or Freiburg forgo the delight of their daily visits to farmers' markets and contacts with vendors, friends or strangers on these market errands. The inhabitants of Antwerp or Strasbourg would not easily be dissuaded from flocking afternoons and evenings to public streets, squares and to the riverfront to enjoy coffee or a meal and the sociability of their fellow citizens. The public realm has not been ruled out of limits, a dangerous place, a zone where caution and vigilance need to be exercised.

In those and many other Western European cities children also enjoy greater freedom and autonomy. They are not always watched or warned against strangers, though are often unobtrusively monitored by familiar adults, especially when present in shared public places, and they receive occasional subtle reminders of how they might play or engage in other activities without impacting on others, particularly the elderly. Here, visits to many Western European cities can be enlightening. In those cities and towns, children still enjoy a greater measure of autonomy, walking to school by themselves, and pursuing diverse agendas alone or with friends.

To North Americans it is always surprising how much freedom of movement young girls especially enjoy, traveling around in their cities and towns by themselves or in pairs until late evening without fear of unpleasantness.

Though rare incidents of violence do occur, against young women in particular, even the massive media attention these receive has not yet altered patterns of behavior of children, and their parents' relative lack of concern.[viii]

We do not wish to leave the impression that all is well with regard to the lives of children and youth in all Western European cities. Many of the larger cities have accommodated the car in ways inimical to children, though public transportation is available to children and is almost always better than in North American cities.

City centers, too, have become largely devoted to commerce, and offer no place for children and youth. Planners for the new center of Berlin certainly have not put children and youth near the top of their agenda. Few children live in the heart of Frankfurt or Vienna.

At the same time, mass housing and strip development surround many of Europe's larger cities. Ugly, and devoid of public places, these unifunctional areas that once characterized Eastern European cities, now surround many Western European cities as well, including those with some of the most intact city centers, such as Paris or Milan. They provide an unhappy habitat for children and a fertile soil for mistrust and aggressiveness, especially among young people.

Nor are some European city dwellers immune from xenophobia; its enactment, however, may be constrained by the considerable presence of ethnic minorities in city streets, squares and parks, on public transportation, (streetcars, buses, etc.) and at many of the city's social events.

How ordinary people react to derision of, and attacks on their fellow citizens is of concern, especially in Germany, where such incidents are much publicized. Civil courage, acting on behalf of those victimized, is important not only for the protection of civil order but also as an example for children and youth. Vigilance is needed for Western European cities and towns to maintain a physical and social fabric that encourages citizens to trust one another.

The child as demon

We cannot conclude a discussion of images and values without calling attention to the idea of the "violent child" that has become fashionable in the media and in public policy discussion.

We have all read about two children, eight and ten years old, who tortured and finally killed a small child in Liverpool, England some years ago; about a six year old boy in Richmond, a city on the San Francisco Bay, who tried to kill his sister; and more recently, among many other incidents, the case of an eight year old Kentucky boy who, together with a young friend, killed a number of his schoolmates with a rifle.

In the case of the six year old Richmond boy, we read that the local district attorney looked into the question whether he could charge a six year old with attempted murder!

Children involved in such violent and destructive behavior are often described as "monsters": the public is outraged and demands severe penalties. Public policy and professional discussions are focused on the violent child, and the phenomenon of "children killing children". Violent acts committed by young people have increased, and so, as we said earlier, has the mistreatment of children. The exposure of children to violence on television, and their practice of violence through participation in electronic games have also seen a dramatic increase.

Too often missing from reactions of outrage is any sense of who is responsible. Unless we believe in "inborn evil", in the "bad seed", we must ask how such violence and destructiveness came about.

All that transforms an infant into a social human being is acquired through exposure to, and interaction with adults, and with the social and physical world that surrounds the child since birth.

We are familiar with studies that document the extreme consequences for infants who are deprived of consistent human contact, of such simple "parenting behavior" as being held, smiled at, shown tenderness and love, and being talked to. The child psychiatrist, Renee Spitz described the damaging effect of the absence of such early bonding behavior with the concept of "hospitalism". Konrad Lorenz supports Spitz's conclusion with examples from animal life, where isolation and neglect of the young animal is almost always fatal.[ix]

It is well documented that language development is connected with how much parents or other adults talk to children, and to how much talk the children hear in their immediate environment. The learning of social behavior (of what to do where and when, and of what not to do), and the learning of social values (of what is "good", "appropriate" and what is "inappropriate" and earns disapproval), involves a very similar process.

All elements of the child's environment, both social and physical, contribute to this learning. The experience and observation of how adults act towards one another are crucial. The behavior of adults to the child then becomes a model for the child. A society that accepts adults who mistreat children, or who use violence towards them, cannot be surprised if children learn to act violently. Communities that ignore, or neglect children, that are not a source of caring and affection for their young (as indeed, animal communities are) likewise cannot be surprised if children lack compassion for others.

And there are, of course, other important sources of social learning, of which exposure to media, especially television, is primary. Here, too, the behavior observed on the screen, despite strenuous denial by the television industry, is a source of social learning.

Equally important for social learning are the qualities of the physical environment, of the neighborhood and of the city, whether meaningful or meaningless, connected or fragmented.

The focus on the "violent child" in public policy debate, and the labeling of children as "young criminals" are examples of how assumptions about others may have serious implications. This "demonization" of children draws attention away from who and what is responsible for teaching them this behavior, such as the failure by parents and the community to socialize and humanize children, their fragmented communities and meaningless physical environments, the preoccupation of media with violence, and the concurrent blurring between "virtual" reality on the computer, and everyday life.

The phrase "the violent child" is particularly insidious because it removes the need to face such complex and difficult questions as who and what is responsible for violent behavior. The image and description of the child as the villain then renders superfluous the need to address the real issues.

[i] One of the basic tenets of the social sciences is W.I. Thomas's proposition that "if situations are defined as real, they will be real in their consequences."

[ii] Leon Eisenberg, *"The Human Nature of Human Nature"* in **Science**, April 1972.

[iii] Sissela Bok, **Mayhem. Violence as Public Entertainment**. Perseus Books, Reading, MA. 1998.

[iv] U.S. Department of Health and Human Services, National Center on Child Abuse and Neglect, *Child Abuse and Neglect: Case Level Data 1993.* Washington DC. US Government Printing Office, 1996.

[v] Jane Jacobs, **The Death and Life of Great American Cities**, New York, Vintage Books, Random House, 1961, p.80

[vi] ibid, p. 82

[vii] It is easy to discern the level of trust and distrust characteristic of the inhabitants of a city. A few years ago one of us was sitting for quite a while at a café on the market place on market day in Tübingen, a German university town of almost 100,000 inhabitants. It so happened that I was writing notes for an earlier book on city life we authored. Next to me was a young man with an infant in a pram. At one point the young man came over and asked "Would you mind watching my son for a little bit while I do some shopping at the market". I readily acceded to the request, and kept an eye on the child while the father did the shopping. When the father returned, however, I pointed out that such a request of a stranger would be highly unusual in a North American city of Tübingen's size. The father replied that while he may have been more hesitant to make this request in a city like Frankfurt or Stuttgart, the general level of trust among citizens of Tübingen was high, and that he really didn't give it much thought, since people shopping at the market often ask their fellow citizens to look after their small children for a brief period.

[viii] In the case of one of the most violent and publicized incidents, the rape and murder of a twelve year old girl, the attacker did not turn out to be a stranger but to be an uncle (discovered through a saliva test).

[ix] Konrad Lorenz, **Der Abbau des Menschlichen**. R. Piper & Co. Verlag, München. 1986

Chapter 8

Society's Ambivalence Towards Children

Despite the rhetoric, children have been forgotten by political leaders, architects, planners, developers and others on whom the fate of our children depends.

A disturbing neglect of children's social and emotional well-being is reflected in the way we have shaped our cities, suburbs and city peripheries. Cities have become centers of commerce, surrounded by housing for the poor and troubled; many children, especially in North America, are confined to suburbs lacking stimulation and variety; other children are warehoused in bleak towers surrounding such European cities as Berlin, Prague, Leipzig, even Paris and Vienna.

What immediately comes to mind is that children have little power to act on their own behalf, to influence social policies, or the actions of politicians, architects, planners and developers.   They have neither economic, nor political power!

The renowned German psychiatrist and social critic Alexander Mitscherlich pointed out that the "commercially oriented planning of our cities is clearly aimed at one group only -- working adults... The world of the child is a sphere of the socially weak, and is ruthlessly manipulated."[i]

While powerlessness and lack of economic utility are important issues, we must still search "deeper" for an explanation of society's treatment of children, which ranges from physical mistreatment, to exclusion of children and youth in the organization and planning of cities and suburbs.

Do we like children?

At our recent international conference on cities the Swiss psychoanalyst and author Arno Gruen suggested that our society does not like children[ii]. Many in the audience agreed with this provocative assertion.

Gruen spoke from his experience in working as a therapist in the United States and in German speaking countries.

A review of how most children are treated in Western countries, and of the social and urban policies impacting children would offer much to support Gruen's statement.

Arno Gruen and the psychoanalyst Alice Miller[iii], view society's attitude towards children not only in political or economic terms, but also as the result of the emotional reaction of adults to their own childhood.

Their work suggests to us that it is to the realm of childhood experience that we must look for the reasons why children are forgotten in urban decision making; that it is, perhaps, this overlooked reaction to personal experience that contributes to the failure of many city officials, architects and planners to identify with children! Their inability to contemplate how the urban environment will adversely impact the lives of children is partly explained by their unwillingness or inability to reexperience their <u>own</u> childhood.

In an important book "Belonging in America" the anthropologist Constance Perrin asks: "If not children, then who is to belong in America?" She summarizes the question and conclusion reached by the Carnegie Council on Children: "Do Americans really like children? Are we the child-centered, child-loving people we claim to be? On just about every issue affecting children's well-being -- health, poverty, intact families, day care, schooling", the Carnegie Council Report concludes, "the decisions adults make in the public domain turn out to be as likely to work against children's interests as for them."iv

Perrin also calls attention to how belatedly the US Congress passed legislation to protect children. "...only after cruelty to animals became fixed in public consciousness did laws extend the same human sensibility to children... Only in 1967 did the Supreme Court explicitly extend to children the same constitutional protections afforded adults, when it established that juveniles are as much protected by the due process clause of the Fourteenth Amendment as adult citizens."[v]

In her book, Perrin also reviews a range of social policies affecting children, among them housing policies that restrict the presence of children in co-ops, condominiums and privately owned housing developments. "About 25 percent of all rental housing and 10 percent of all cooperatives and condominiums do not now permit people below the age of 18 to live in them."[vi]

Attitudes towards youth

Teenagers receive unfavorable attention from adults. Referring to the irrationality of adults in their relations to teenagers, Perrin does not mince words: "Towards teenagers, denial is the favorite: they just aren't there, so there's no need to make a place for them in the community or the economy before they arrive full-grown. Still minors, belonging to no part of the adult world, some adolescents are left with little choice but to make up worlds of their own, as gang members, shopping mall 'rats', drug takers, drop-outs, and incipient alcoholics. Pushed out to the edge, they retreat into their province of cardom, until their isolated frenzy kills them (and some adults) on their roads to nowhere."[vii]

In reviewing Herb Gans' classic study of Levittown, one of the first planned US suburbs, the sociologist Ray Oldenburg writes: "The adults of Levittown maintained a world in which youth were so shut out that no one seemed to know them. During Gans's study many bizarre rumors about the adolescents and their behavior floated among the adults and were widely believed. One rumor had it that forty-four of the high school senior girls were pregnant. Gans checked. There were two who were pregnant, and one of them was about to get married. The estrangement of the generations that made such rumors believable also brought hostility. Levittown's youth grew up to dislike adults generally, engaged in considerable vandalism, and began consuming considerable amounts of alcohol."[viii]

Mistreatment of children

A considerable increase in child abuse and neglect has been reported in a number of studies such as the National Incidence Study of Child Abuse and Neglect. This study, based in part on reports from community professionals, teachers, social workers and law enforcement officials shows that the incidence of child abuse and neglect doubled during the period 1986 - 1993. According to the study, the number of mistreated children rose from 1.4 million in 1986 to 2.9 million in 1993, and has remained over 3 million since then[ix]. Almost ninety percent of those responsible for the mistreatment were the victims' parents or other relatives. According to the National Incidence Study, the number of children who were injured has increased from 143,000 to 572,000 in 1993.

While the methods used in the National Study may have inflated the number of children involved, several states did not provide information on this subject.

A recent (1998) CNN special report estimated that every day at least six children die as a result of mistreatment in the home.

Until fairly recently physicians and law enforcement officials were reluctant to implicate and accuse parents in cases of injured children. Some countries such as Germany do not, as far as we know, gather national statistics on this issue, though there are frequent media reports on serious parental abuse. Swiss newspapers, on the other hand, until fairly recently did not print information on child abuse involving parents.

Lack of public concern

Whatever the precise data on the actual extent of child mistreatment, the number of children involved is alarming!

It is, therefore, surprising that, in a recent survey by the Harvard School of Public Health (1997) Americans did not think child abuse was a major social problem (compared to their concern with drug abuse).

A steady flow of reports of parents torturing, imprisoning, maiming, or even killing their children can be found in the American press and other media. In a recent review of reported cases of serious child abuse (resulting in serious injury or death) in the Chicago Tribune covering the year 1997, 304 articles were found. Newspaper reports of child mistreatment can, of course, also be found in the press of many countries.

Why then, do these reports not lead to a sense of outrage and alarm on the part of parents who, as we have discussed earlier, are in the main concerned with danger to their children from "strangers".

Perhaps some explanation can be found in a U.S. study, reported by Perrin, based on a national probability sample, where parents, both men and women, were asked to report "...on their acts of 'physical force and violence' within the single previous year. The fact that parents were willing to report their behavior indicated to these investigators that 'many of our subjects did not consider kicking, biting, punching, beating up, shooting or stabbing their children deviant. In other words, they may have admitted to these acts because they felt they were acceptable or tolerable ways of bringing up children.'"[x]

Significance of childhood experience

Many parents justify punishment and violence to children on the basis of their own experience, and think they were not the worse for it.

The work of Swiss psychoanalyst Alice Miller, developed in her six books, represents a powerful critique of professionals and the public regarding their lack of attention to the mistreatment of children.

Her contribution lies in her conclusion that children are mistreated and abused on a much larger scale than is admitted, and that this mistreatment and abuse results in destructiveness both on an individual and societal level.

She believes that repression of the intolerable pain of mistreatment in one's past becomes the basis for subsequent failures to recognize, identify and empathize with the pain inflicted on children by parental lack of understanding, or by physical and emotional mistreatment. "Parents (adults) who have never known love, who on coming into the world met with coldness, insensitivity, indifference and blindness and whose entire childhood and youth were spent in this atmosphere, are unable to bestow love... Nevertheless their children will survive. And like their parents they too will not remember the torments to which they were once exposed because those torments ... have all been repressed, that is, completely banished from consciousness."[xi]

To Alice Miller, as to Freud, the attitudes and behavior of parents towards children are important for human development, but she goes beyond Freud in claiming mistreatment of children as the single most critical factor in the creation of social ills.

For this book, Miller's work is relevant in at least two respects. One, we can infer from her thesis that the destructive behavior of city dwellers (aggression, violence, drug and alcohol abuse) have their source in the mistreatment and abuse of children. These childhood experiences also contribute to the climate of distrust and suspicion prevalent among city dwellers.

And secondly, she makes clear that without a major shift in the quality of parent-child relationships, without a reduction in punitive and abusive parenting, such socially troubling patterns as addiction and youth violence will continue, and escalate.

It should be mentioned that there are, as the reader knows, many people who see the origin of destructive behavior in "too humane" models of child rearing. Among those who believe in the dangers of permissive child rearing we also find the advocates of physical punishment and stricter penalties for young offenders.

In learning about societies and cities characterized by a relative lack of social pathology we find strong community bonds, and parents who cherish their children and childhood. Being "good" to one's children is greatly valued. In those cultures, for example, maternal behavior by fathers -- being with, taking care of, enjoying contact with their children -- receives approbation and praise from other community members.

Failure to identify with the city's children

Over many years we have observed the ambivalence of political leaders, urban professionals, architects, planners and developers when it comes to considering the effects of their policies, decisions, urban structures, projects, or organization of traffic on the lives of their city's children.

Since the inception of the International Making Cities Livable Conferences in 1985 we have organized panel sessions on the "Good City for Children" in each of our biannual conferences. These sessions usually were not well attended when scheduled at the same time as other more fashionable subjects.

Frequently, a series of questions was formulated to guide discussion and generate participant response. Questions included: what features of their city do the assembled urban leaders and professionals consider "good" for children, and in what respects are their cities inimical or hostile to children. All too frequently, response to these questions was minimal, reflecting how little thought had been given by urban decision makers to the issues affecting children.

When we inquired about the last occasion when there was a serious discussion of the impact on lives of children of a pending plan, or project in their city, few could recall such an occasion, or the specifics of the discussion.

We should add that our participants, like many other political leaders and urban professionals, express great concern with children, and we have no reason to doubt their sincerity. But when they do cite projects or plans in answer to these questions they almost always speak about something that is being done especially for children, such as a playground, a community center, or a children's museum. Where they are unable to identify with children is in how every aspect of the city's urban design, built fabric, organization of streets, or architectural forms will be experienced by children, and how almost everything that is constructed impacts on children!

---

i   Alexander Mitscherlich, **Die Unwirtlichkeit Unserer Städte**, Frankfurt am Main, Suhrkamp Verlag, 1969.
ii   Arno Gruen, paper at the 17th International Making Cities Livable Conference, Freiburg, Germany, September 5-9, 1995

[iii]   Alice Miller resigned her membership in psychoanalytic societies for their failure to recognize the dangers to children of parental and educational practices.

[iv]   Constance Perrin, **Belonging in America**, University of Wisconsin Press, 1988, p. 160

[v]   Ibid. pp. 165, 161

[vi]   Ibid. pp. 161.

[vii]   Ibid. p. 170

[viii]   Ray Oldenburg, **The Great Good Place**, New York, Paragon House, 1991, pp. 268-9

[ix]   Arianne Huffington, **How to Overthrow the Government**, Regan Books, Harper Collins, 2000.

[x]   Constance Perrin, op.cit., pp. 165-6

[xi]   Alice Miller, **Breaking Down the Wall of Silence**, Meridian, Penguin Books USA, NY, 1993.

Chapter 9

Social Capital
and Social Investment
in Children

Social capital

Social capital, as defined by Robert Putnam, refers to features of social life, "social networks, norms and trust that enable participants to act together more effectively." Civic engagement, caring and supportive behaviors are related. These features of social life are the "glue" that connects and sustains members of a community.

We suggest that the idea of social capital is equally relevant to the relationship between the community, parents and children. The community, and its agents, the parents, must either build up a transgenerational social capital of trust, of love and caring, or face the consequences of indifference and mistreatment.

Situations in which children are neglected or mistreated by their parents or by their community, represent for the family therapist Nagy a mortgaging or a "borrowing from the funds of the future."

When investment in social capital diminishes, as Putnam claims, a sense of community declines. And a decline in both is especially worrisome in relation to the lives of children.

If the studies documenting an increase in child mistreatment and child neglect during the past two decades are correct -- and we believe they are -- then we may expect that when these children grow up the pattern of mistreatment will further increase.

As Alice Miller writes: "A human being born into a cold, indifferent world will regard his situation as the only possible one. Everything that person later comes to believe, advocate, and deem right is founded on his first formative experiences."[i]

Lack of investment in children

Some urban environments, neglected inner city schools, deteriorating public housing projects, and derelict neighborhoods are analogous to parental mistreatment.

Children in many of America's city centers go to neglected, ugly schools, live in equally inhospitable housing, walk through neighborhoods of empty lots and car parks, and streets with bars and liquor stores on many corners. They have little access to areas of their city that offer a more intact and interesting urban environment. The picture is quite familiar to all of us, though we do not experience it with the eyes of a child. The world in which these children grow up can be described as "loveless", insensitive and inhospitable!

Children living in tower blocks on the periphery of cities, around European as well as North American cities, face a similarly inhospitable environment.

Paradoxically, children in suburbs and gated communities also do not fare much better. While individual houses and schools are considerably more pleasant, the suburban environment is bland and homogeneous. Except for the commercial shopping malls little thought or resources are devoted to providing a stimulating environment for suburban children.

Mistrust of the Public Realm

Fear of others has also been carried to the new environment to which parents have moved to escape the city. Parents prefer to keep children at home before television and computer, or occupied with video games. Some parents purchase expensive play and exercise equipment to induce children to stay at home, away from communal places, of which, indeed, there are few in suburbia.

It is crucial to identify those social processes that increase social capital, and that reverse the downward trends of mistrust, isolation and aggression.

Attention must be given to increasing multifunctional use of streets and public urban places, and the variety of social events that facilitate contact, trust and confirmation. On the other hand, physical and social elements that discourage public social life -- homogeneity, unifunctional areas, empty spaces, discontinuity in the urban fabric -- need to be discouraged in the remaking of our cities.

Conflict and the public realm

We should correct the misunderstanding that the public realm is desirable only if it involves the absence of unpleasantness and conflict. If people are in each others presence on a regular basis, and these are persons from different backgrounds, with diverse life styles, different "ways of being in the world", they will at times irritate, and seem troublesome to one another.

They may challenge each other's prejudices about how one should behave, and how persons should relate to each other. At its best, the encounter with the strange and unfamiliar, in the words of the theologian Paul Tillich, "leads to questions and serves to elevate reason to ultimate significance"[ii].

There are a variety of attitudes and reactions towards others whom we encounter in the public realm. For example, some people are sympathetic to young persons who look different (e.g. wear earrings, paint their hair or face, or wear special costumes); they may recall their own adolescent efforts to establish their own mode of dress, and show understanding of the efforts of the young to join a peer group through appropriate costuming or public social behavior. Yet, other adults view such "different" young persons with intolerance, fear, even with loathing. Even children may reflect their parents' prejudices or contempt for them.

A much better understanding of the positive, inclusive function of public places and the public realm is needed on the part of city dwellers, so that exaggerated concerns and fears do not shut out a variety of people, especially the young, from sharing the public world.

Many of the reactions of those troubled by the presence of the "alienated" youth can be attributed to this misunderstanding that social life in public should be "conflict free", that the least kind of "otherness" -- a challenge to homogeneity -- is a threat.

While public urban places can reveal latent negative attitudes and emotions, they can also, if well located and well designed, provide the social context in which city dwellers learn to accept and live with those different from themselves. At best such places may become catalysts for mutual understanding, learning and social healing.

A society that celebrates diversity, the co-presence of young and old, persons of different ethnic origins and with different life styles takes the first step towards becoming an inclusive community!

Conclusion

If we take seriously the idea of the city as analogous to a biological organism, then the city, like every organism, exhibits self-regulating properties. Older cities such as Venice or Siena, which have evolved over time, exhibit these self-healing properties. Foremost among them are: a physical fabric that is not chaotic and fragmented; a range of public places and streets that stimulate an active social life and serve as focal points for dialogue and conversation; and a range of community events, whether public markets, town meetings, festivals or celebrations. All these places and events are inclusive not exclusive, permitting and involving the widest possible participation of young and old, well to do and poor, native and stranger.

[i] Alice Miller, **Breaking Down the Wall of Silence**, New York, Meridian, Penguin Books, 1993

[ii] Paul Tillich, cited in Jane Jacobs, **The Death and Life of Great American Cities,** New York, Random House, 1961, p. 238.

Chapter 10

Connecting the Worlds of Children and Adults

How can children become involved in the life of their community? How can they develop a sense that their contribution to the community is appreciated and valued? In what kind of events can children participate and enjoy being with community members of all ages?

Children and youth have been separated from the adult world of work, commerce, even leisure. Sharing a common world has become difficult. Even spending time with children is considered a "chore" by some adults. Children soon learn that they are not valued by adults, and not included in their world!

In communities that place value on childhood, adults enjoy spending time with children; both adults and children feel confirmed in this intergenerational exchange.

In these communities many events and activities have evolved that attract the participation of young and old, that give children a clear message that their contributions are valued, and that unite the generations in celebration.

The examples given here may appear mundane, but it is just these commonplace events, taken for granted by many city dwellers as part of their everyday life, that provide valuable lessons. Many of the examples given here are based on repeated personal observation in European cities.

Festivals

Festivity and celebration are essential to human life. More than any other activity, community festivals provide the opportunity for children and young people to play valued roles, and to share with adults delight, laughter and joy that bind the community together.

Festivals are an organizing and unifying force in the life of a city. They bring people together in a different spirit from that prevailing in everyday social life.

"The festival", Harvey Cox proposes, "is a distinctly human activity. It arises from man's peculiar power to incorporate into his own life the joys of other people and the experience of previous generations... The very essence of celebration is participation and equality, the abolition of domination and paternalism."[i]

Successful community festivals permit neighbors, friends and strangers, old and young to work, eat, talk, dance and sing with one another. Genuine community festivals are diminishing, even in European cities where they existed for many centuries. It is instructive, therefore, to learn from examples where they have been maintained.

Being part of the community

For many children participation in a festival marks their induction into the life of the community. In the festivals of Palio, in Siena, and the flower festival of Cannara, children begin to prepare for their role when only three or four years old. At festival processions, children are often at, or close to the head.

Adolescents play important roles in many festivals. They display skill and strength, such as tossing and catching flags, as in Palio; they play traditional rhythms on pipe and drum, as in the Basel Fasnacht; or they perform together a complex ritual, as in the "Ceri" festival in Gubbio, where runners compete in a steep course up hill while carrying heavy wooden figures. In all cases, their roles require much practice.

Those who participated in previous years are role models, overseeing the festival and passing on skills and experience.

It is important to note that genuine community festivals are not a one or two day event. Months, even years are spent in preparation and practice

Playing a valued role

The meaning of Palio for the social life of Siena extends far beyond the race. The festival provides a reason for intense social involvement within the neighborhood, and a focus around which many community activities revolve. It is also a way to show children and young people that they are highly valued.

From the earliest age little children learn how to play the drum, wave and toss their neighborhood flag. At around five years old, after much practice and coaching from parents and siblings, they become proficient enough to participate in Palio. Dressed in historic costume, they often lead processions through the city.

Some adolescents and youths are selected to enact historic dignitaries, others provide the procession's climax with sophisticated drum rhythms and ever higher and more complex flag tossing ensembles.

At community festivals individual skills are usually not pitted against each other in competition, but rather displayed for the appreciation of all. It is hoped that every individual will excel, so that the whole community may share in a sense of pride.

Learning to coordinate efforts

All community festivals exercise collaborative skills. Children and young people learn how to act as a team to achieve the common goal.

The festival of the "Ceri" in Gubbio illustrates this. The three "Ceri" are elaborately carved wooden structures like elongated spires, about thirty feet high. At the top of one is the figure of the Virgin Mary; atop the others are patron saints. The "Ceri" are mounted on a horizontal base designed to permit a team of young men to carry it on their shoulders.

Each "Ceri" is the proud emblem of one of the many community associations. At the festival teams of young men from each society race with their Ceri through the narrow streets of Gubbio, up the steep hillside to a chapel above the town.

This race is repeated the following week with smaller Ceri, carried by boys aged ten to twelve; and again a week later, with very small Ceri carried by little boys.

Creating beauty

The coordinated effort of all members of the community -- children, young people and adults -- often produces an object of great beauty, and everyone takes pride in the part they played.

The festival of Corpus Domini, as celebrated in Cannara, Italy, with a continuous carpet of flowers around the town, is one of the most genuine community festivals in Europe, and involves the participation of all ages.

It takes several months for each street to decide on the designs, prepare drawings, collect and process the flowers. Women and children collect flowers from the fields; even very small children concentrate for hours beside their mothers and grandmothers, plucking petals and preparing boxes of variegated colors.

At eight or nine in the evening before the festival the flower petal carpets begin to take shape. Everyone gets down on hands and knees in their street, little children next to their grandparents, teenagers and adults, men and women. Toddlers who can barely walk help to fill in the petal designs.

Some children get sleepy and are put to bed, but everyone else works through the night, reinforced by a midnight spaghetti dinner, until the carpet is finished. When morning comes a few streets are still finishing the last details, while the children are energetically starting new carpets with the left over petals. Before the procession visitors and neighbors walk around to admire each street's carpet.

Eating and drinking together

Eating and drinking together is an essential part of any community festival, and this provides opportunity for community members, including young people, to collaborate in preparing food, serving, and cleaning up as well as celebrating together.

Siena's low rate of delinquency, crime, and drug abuse has been attributed to the strength of its community life, which ensures that all children and young people feel included.

During the week before Palio each competing neighborhood prepares a feast on their main street or square for the night before the race. Up to one thousand people, children, adolescents, young and old, may eat and celebrate together until late into the night. Community members help in the kitchen, set up, and clear tables.

This is not a unique event. In fact, since each neighborhood has its own community kitchen in their community center, neighborhood feasts may be organized many times a year.

In 1990 when we organized an International Making Cities Livable Conference in Siena during the week before we were invited to join the dinners of the Onda and Lupo Contradas, sitting together at long trestle tables, under brightly lit lanterns shaped in the contrada symbols.

Children, parents and grandparents sat together, and some extra tables were set up for toddlers and very young children supervised by adolescents; but very soon they were playing around the adults.

The meals had been prepared by contrada members, both men and women (occasionally meals are catered by restaurants in the contrada), and the young contrada members served.

Weaving together the strands of the community

Many community festivals involve processions. The purpose of the procession is to weave together the different strands of the community. Representatives of all groups participate, and the route leads through different areas of the city. Sometimes neighborhood processions converge in the city center.

The Basel Fasnacht (Carnival) is one of the most successful community festivals held in larger cities. Unique to Fasnacht are the hundreds of societies, or "cliques", to which Baselers belong. The cliques meet for various activities throughout the year, but their main purpose is to organize their participation in Fasnacht.

Each clique selects a theme -- usually political satire -- and for many months members convene to design and make costumes, write satirical poems, build lantern floats illustrating their theme, and practice pipe and drum music. In some of the larger cliques the children select their own particular theme (e.g. making fun of school, pop stars, etc..) Some groups practice a special form of jazz, "Guggenmusik" that delights all, but especially children.

Processions continue for three days, during which time business is forgotten, and work gives way to music and merriment. After months of planning and preparation the festival provides an opportunity for constant, serendipitous and unstructured sociability as thousands of people old and young, children and teenagers, mill the streets, both in and out of costume, looking for friends and neighbors, teasing and being teased, flirting, joking, and making nonsense.

Farmers markets

Genuine farmers markets, where farmers from the surrounding countryside sell their own produce, are very successful in drawing children and adults together, and appeal to all ethnic groups, well to do and less well off. At least for the duration of the market the square or street is free from traffic, therefore safe for children; and the setting, preferably the most beautiful place in the city, enhances the experience.

For children the variety of produce on display provides a fascinating cornucopia of colors, shapes, textures, smells and tastes, gratifying all of the senses. They learn about the bounty of nature, an intensely satisfying and pleasurable experience.

Street performers

Musicians and other performers in public places are valuable catalysts for social life, prompting spontaneous conversation among their audience of old and young. Some performers encourage audience participation: jugglers throw a ball to a child; clowns enlist a member of the audience into their act; mimics turn unwitting passersby into performers, and thereby heighten the drama of urban social life.

Street entertainers demonstrate to children that adults have not lost their delight in the absurd, their ability to react spontaneously, to step out of themselves, to laugh at themselves - qualities which endear them to children and create a bond between young and old.

Street entertainers are very much part of the daily life of some European cities, especially where volume of traffic and traffic noise has been reduced.

Antwerp, Belgium, for example, is a city very hospitable to street entertainers. A variety of musicians and performers can always be found on Handschoenmarkt and Groenplaats, two of the major traffic free city squares. We observed frequently how street entertainers related to children in those places. One example, "Dis Jokkies", the jocular jazz band from Breda in the

Netherlands, mesmerized the crowds one Saturday afternoon. After playing together for a while, they dispersed among the crowd, each musician serenading different onlookers, and three musicians got down on their knees to play to the toddlers, encouraging them to approach and touch the instruments.

Beautifying the neighborhood

Festivals are not the only events that provide young people an opportunity to combine fun with playing a valued role. As artists in North America have demonstrated, children and young people can also participate in creating public art to enhance their city.

In San Francisco's Mission District, a strongly Hispanic neighborhood, resident artists have been at work for decades creating over a hundred magnificent murals that celebrate the Hispanic and native Indian heritage. Several of these artists involve young community members, particularly on projects in schools, and community gardens.

One San Francisco artist, Ruth Asawa, has worked with children to create several murals, but perhaps her most interesting collaborative work, created with the participation of one hundred children, is the bronze fountain celebrating San Francisco on the steps of the Hyatt Union Square Hotel. Images of the city, cable cars, Victorian houses, boats, bridges and seagulls, modeled in baker's clay by the children, were cast in bronze by the artist, and combined to create a relief collage on the fountain.

Play in the city

Children's need for play, for experimentation, for laughter, for touching, climbing, tasting, for fantasy and imagination, is sorely limited by the functional character of the modern city that provides neither places, nor the natural props for spontaneous play.

Children use play as a way of understanding the world, testing reality, exploring the physical character of materials or objects, and learning how to change their environment. What makes their experimentation fun is to use objects in unintended ways, to transform reality into an imaginary landscape, to create worlds that are within, and parallel to the adult world, but require the passport of imagination.

Twentieth century planning, with its overemphasis on functionality and order, sets apart segregated zones -- playgrounds -- for the unruly activity of children's play. By their rigid and unimaginative character, playgrounds transform "play" into physical activity devoid of fantasy and experimentation.

"The average American city child" observes Rudofsky, "gets his first bad taste of the drearier forms of play in the confining space of a playground where the so-called playground furniture has been set up for taming him -- concrete bunkers and metal cages, abstractions of the modern city, the nearest approximation to his future Lebensraum current artistry and design philosophy will permit. He is expected to hop from rung to rung like a pet bird, or whiz along mazes that won't tax a mouse's brain."[ii]

Of course, the child is learning something all the time. For example, he learns that children and adults exist in different worlds, that only toddlers in the sandbox can share their world with adults; that the playground will exercise his muscles, but not his imagination; that the world is hard and impervious, and does not permit him to make his own impression on it (if he tries, it is considered vandalism). And he learns, in Richard Dattner's words, "that the man-made world is dull, ugly, and dangerous, and empty of sensuous satisfactions; that civilization delights in reducing the varied potentials and unique qualities of individuals to a pattern of uniformity."[iii]

The city as playground

Sandboxes, swings and slides inside chain link fences are no substitute for playing on a traffic free street where children can be part of the everyday life of the city. Ideally, the whole city should be usable as a playground.

Given the opportunity, children use every detail of their environment as stimulus to their imaginative games. Doorways and thresholds provide a convenient niche for games with cards and toys; a pattern of stone paving is transformed into a landscape for a game with bottletops and marbles; a window sill is used for a game of flipping discs.

In the city-as-playground children redefine street furniture -- steps, walls, bollards, posts and rails -- as elements in their play, as home base or goal post; and sections of public urban places come to be identified with particular games -- football in one corner, skipping near the cafe, tag in the center, swapping cards and stamps at the steps.

All of these activities occur within sight of adults carrying on their daily lives, and the child is free to move back and forth between play, and a playful interaction with adults -- and indeed, those adults present may become involved in their play.

Connecting the worlds

To paraphrase Mumford, much damage has been inflicted on modern society by specialization, fragmentation, social segregation, tribalism and overcultivation of favorite functions. Children have been the foremost victims of these developments.

To reconnect children and youth with their fellow city dwellers is not a utopian task but rather one of remembering, and reinventing those social events and occasions when children were participants and partners in a common world. But it will require renewed attention to the public realm of our cities, to make the public places and streets hospitable and accessible to adults and children!

[i]   Harvey Cox, **The Feast of Fools,** Cambridge, MA, Harvard University Press, 1969, p. 7.
[ii]   Bernard Rudofsky, **Streets for People**, New York, Doubleday & Company Inc. 1969, p.328.
[iii]   Richard Dattner, **Design for Play**.

Chapter 11

Information Technology and Children

Hundreds if not thousands of schools in North America lack the basic amenities to make them hospitable and stimulating environments for the six to seven hours a day that children spend in school.

Many school systems have reallocated resources in response to the advocacy and sometimes pressure from promoters of the new information technologies. Schools have canceled art, music and drama programs to support the purchase and upkeep of computers.

While school administrators hearken to the mantra "a computer for every child", schools deteriorate. The curtailment of educational enrichment offered by music and arts programs -- especially for children whose parents cannot compensate for the deficit -- leaves a permanent vacuum at a time in their lives when the stimulation of aesthetic, artistic and creative sensibilities is most likely to have enduring impact.

In this light we wonder about a political agenda that demands a computer, with access to the internet, for every child, while neglecting other more basic aspects of children's well-being!

Unintended consequences

We know from past experience that every new technology is at first over promoted. It should be obvious that new technologies always carry both benefits and risks. There is always too little attention to the long term, unintended, but nonetheless real consequences of each new technology. Few anticipated that the automobile could damage the natural landscape and alter the life of city inhabitants, but the overwhelming accommodation to the needs of the automobile has been a major obstacle to making cities hospitable and livable.[i] Nuclear technology is another example where initially, scientists did not anticipate the significant risks to humans and to the ecology as a consequence of radiation and problems of nuclear waste disposal.[ii]

The new drug technologies presented many similar lessons. Their promoters downplayed their danger and long term effects. One of the numerous dramatic examples was the promotion of the drug Thalidomide as a sedative for women. The drug was marketed to women with the slogan "safe enough for babies".[iii] Early warnings by German physicians about the potential dangers of Thalidomide (marketed as Contergan in Germany) were disregarded. It was realized only later that those responsible for introducing the drug had omitted to examine drug effects on fetal development, resulting in thousands of deformed children.[iv]

We should keep examples such as these in mind to understand that the effects of each new technology are multiple and complex. In the case of the new information technologies, they may affect the lives of children in unanticipated ways, and be detrimental to their emotional health.

We should heed Neil Postman's warning: "The role that new technology should play in schools or anywhere else is something that needs to be discussed without the hyperactive fantasies of cheerleaders. In particular, the computer and its associated technologies are awesome additions to a culture... But like all important technologies of the past, they are Faustian bargains, giving and taking away, sometimes in equal measure, sometimes more in one way than the other. It is strange - indeed, shocking - that with the twenty-first century so close, we can still talk of new technologies as if they were unmixed blessings -- gifts, as it were, from the gods."[v]

Advocates of new technologies often claim side effects to be trivial, or unimportant. They also argue that proliferation of the new information technology is inevitable, whatever possible adverse consequences.

There was little debate about the conclusion of a major study of the social and psychological effects of internet use at home. Researchers at Carnegie Mellon University found that "people who spend even a few hours a week on line experience higher levels of depression and loneliness than if they used the computer network less frequently."[vi]

We all share a responsibility to consider seriously the social and even moral implications of this technology, especially when it is hailed as ushering in a new millennium in the history of mankind, and when it will affect every facet of our lives, especially the lives of children.

The claim is made that the computer age will spawn new human beings (cyborgs) connected to each other through electronic means,[vii] and lead to a new vision of mankind and the universe.

History has demonstrated that human beings are infinitely adaptable. They have survived under the most contrived conditions and inhospitable habitats. But the question still needs to be asked: "What price has been paid for the promised benefits! What functions have been atrophied! In what respects were human beings diminished!"

Carl Gustav Jung pointed out how essential it is to face the "shadow", the other, or dark side of our selves. For the promoters of this new technology the shadow of their enterprise may be the wish to be seen as pioneers and benefactors while reaping enormous profits. There is a reluctance, perhaps a "devil may care" attitude to considering the potential harmful effects.

"What will technologies that alter our sense of reality mean, in the long run?" asks Mark Slouka in an entertaining and insightful critique. "What will they do to us? No one knows. Ask the techno-visionaries how human beings (who have evolved over millions of years in response to the constraints and pressures of the physical world) might respond to existence in aphysical environments, and they'll fall over one another in their willingness to admit that they have no idea. Does this concern them just a little? Frighten them, maybe? Not a bit. "The best things in life are scary" Kevin Kelly told me recently, "I'm serious." Unfortunately for the rest of us, he probably is. So we go on, blindfolded, pedal to the floor, over the canyonlands."[viii]

Finally, some grave concerns are voiced! A vision of the awesome powers of the new technologies has recently been advanced by Bill Joy, co-founder of Sun Microsystems, who also helped to create the "computer languages known as Unix, Java and Jini, which are the basic fabric of today's networked world." He warned an audience of America's leading technologists about the potential dangers to human existence that not paying attention to the serious risks of their creations (all based on digital information technologies) would entail.

The risks we are concerned with in this book are on a more modest scale, but they potentially involve risks to young human beings and they need our attention and analysis.

Computer limits of interpersonal contact

We are being persuaded that individuals who communicate by typing messages on the internet constitute an electronic "agora", analogous to the public meeting place of the ancient Greeks! We are expected to accept that "community" on the computer replicates the real thing.

Communication in cyberspace lacks the face-to-face, immediate encounter of person to person. When we speak with people in face-to-face settings there is a great deal of information available to evaluate the meaning and intent of their words. We observe facial expression, body posture and body movements. We hear volume, inflection, timbre and tone of voice. We receive many cues about social and cultural background; and importantly, we overlap in real time -- that is, we are witness to a response while we speak, and can modify or adjust our communication accordingly.

We must not overlook the significant difference between contact and communication among persons in real life, and on the computer. Of course much information can be exchanged on the computer. It is also useful to keep in touch with people. But real life contact enables us to experience each other – to exist in an authentic relationship where each feels and reacts to the full impact of the other's presence, where an interpersonal (zwischenmenschlich) bond is created, as Martin Buber puts it, or where, in the language of the vanished counter culture, each is exposed to the "vibes" of the other.

This is not to say that while transmitting messages via the computer among family members, friends or workmates each is not able to conjure up (from his or her past) the experience of the other's presence. But this is only useful when a real, authentic relationship already exists. To approximate the feeling of a real I-Thou interpersonal encounter on the computer would be especially difficult for children if no groundwork for differentiated personal relationships has been laid.

Failure to comprehend "meta-communication"

It is quite possible that children and young people who spend a great deal of time with this technology, will find it more difficult to become competent and skilled in interacting with diverse other persons. Communicating on the internet they do not experience the fact that human interaction occurs on many levels and in many modalities; and that these modalities may qualify the messages sent, be incongruous, or explicitly contradict them.[ix] Expression and recognition of subtle forms of human communication, especially irony, sarcasm, and humor involve more than one communicational modality (e.g. facial expression, body posture, tone of voice). It is frequently the incongruity among these different modalities that conveys the more subtle message. Will the expression and understanding of more subtle forms of human exchange diminish?

Communicating approval and love

Perhaps more importantly, we should recognize that all persons, but especially children, require confirmation, and that children become anxious if they don't receive esteem and approbation from significant adults.

Love, affection, approval -- confirmation of self esteem -- are frequently communicated, especially for children and young people, by non-verbal means, by touch, facial expression, tone of voice, a smile, a pat, an embrace, a kind word softly spoken! A hypothesis widely accepted throughout the social sciences is that "people's behavior is shaped or affected by the esteem that others give to them or withdraw from them". ˣ

Our concern is: how do children get a sense of their value and worth from communication on the internet? There are clear limits to computer communication as a substitute for conveying esteem, approbation, and confirmation of one's worth, especially for younger children.

The wish of every person for confirmation, to the philosopher Martin Buber, is the basis of social life. To the extent to which communication with young people is channeled through a medium that does not allow for the expression of confirmation or affection, to this extent their sense of self worth will suffer!

Social and attitudinal learning and information technology

Social learning ordinarily occurs through observation and imitation of adults skilled in relating to other human beings. One's family is one source of this learning. However, learning from one's family alone does not enable children to acquire the skills required to relate to the wide range of human beings who now populate our cities. Societies and cities are becoming very diverse, whether in North America or Europe. Children and young people have to learn how to relate to individuals of different backgrounds, how to make contact, to understand each other.

Not only that! Children need to have models of responsible behavior. What models of social interaction, of supportive and helpful behavior, of acts of responsibility of one person toward another are provided by the world of cyberspace? Just consider what can be learned by a child as an observer of "real life" human contact? In real life, if an elderly person stumbles, one may observe her being picked up and helped by a bystander; or a child may observe an adult showing concern for a young person in distress. By observing acts of responsibility or compassion a child learns ways of relating to others. How much attitudinal learning is possible in the virtual world?

Before the advent of information technology, Jane Jacobs, the wise student of city life, had pointed out that it is only in real life experience in shared public places that essential social learning may occur. "In real life, only from the ordinary adults of the city sidewalks do children learn -- if they learn at all -- the first fundamentals of successful city life; people must take a modicum of responsibility for each other even if they have no ties to each other. This is a lesson nobody learns by being told... it is a folly to build cities in a way that wastes this normal casual manpower for child rearing and... leaves this essential job undone -- with terrible consequences."[xi]..

Socialization by the mouse

It is in the "real" city that children are socialized to become full community members by participating in the life of their city, by being with diverse people, young and old, similar and dissimilar from themselves. They learn human competencies and social skills through contact with diverse people; and they learn about caring, responsibility and trust by observation and participation in everyday social life. It is especially instructive for children to witness acts of civil courage and civic engagement.

We are not ready to disregard the role of the community in favor of an ideology that is willing to replace the presence of real people in real social settings with "socialization by the mouse".

Deuterolearning

Most social learning involves what Bateson has termed "deuterolearning" -- learning how to learn. For children especially, any participation in cooperative and collaborative activity, whether in the preparation or staging of a community event, festival or celebration, becomes the basis for working together with others, children and adults alike, in a wide range of endeavors.

This kind of deuterolearning is always the latent objective of many drama, dance, and music programs that involve young persons (often young persons at risk) to lay a foundation of working together in an enjoyable effort. While some forms of collaboration (perhaps co-writing a play) are possible in cyberspace, the complex collaboration involved in performing a play is not possible "on line".

Raising these questions does not make light of the many uses of information technology for commercial and scientific purposes, data access or retrieval. Children need to learn to avail themselves of these opportunities.

In this chapter we have considered a few of the broader consequences of a new technology that affects the range of human behavior and social processes. We are skeptical of those who pronounce cyberspace a virtual city, capable of serving all of the functions of a real city for its inhabitants, especially of its children.

Electronic violence

One of the unanticipated consequences that we spoke of earlier in relation to new technologies, e.g. the new information technology, is the development of electronic games that expose children to violence.

Two concurrent and mutually reinforcing factors have resulted in the immersion of children in a culture of violence. The development and marketing of electronic games could only be so successful because the fear and distrust of other human beings (see Chapter 7) led parents to withdraw their children from the public realm of neighborhoods and public places where they could spend time with adults, and observe how to live with, and take responsibility for one another.

In withdrawing their children to what they consider the safety of their home they increased their exposure to, and consequent seduction into the world of TV, computer and electronic games.

In 1993 a Commission of the American Psychological Association concluded that "There is absolutely no doubt that higher levels of viewing violence on television are correlated with increased acceptance of aggressive attitudes and increased aggressive behavior... Children's exposure to violence in the mass media, particularly at young ages, can have harmful lifelong consequences. Aggressive habits learned early on in life are the foundation for later behavior."[xii] Much of what children see and learn about the world from TV and electronic games can be aptly described by Sissela Bok's term "mayhem"[xiii].

In a rapid development since 1993 electronic games have become a feature of "home entertainment" for children. According to Naisbitt[xiv], electronic games selling violence account for seventy percent of the market. If watching TV has induced children to fear being kidnapped, what about an electronic world where violence predominates!

Some children are attracted, even addicted to violence and destructiveness which, most unfortunately, in some instances is acted out. An example of this is the two Littleton boys who were addicted to violent electronic games. Naisbitt reports that the two teenage boys "were immersed in America's culture of violence delivered through television, films, the Internet, stereo systems, and electronic games such as Doom, which they played for hours daily, including a personalized version of the game that one of the boys had modified to match the corridors of his high school, Columbine."[xv]

Elsewhere in this book we suggest some of the familial dynamics that lay the foundation for the expression of aggression and violence.

But it is the immersion and exposure to this culture of electronic violence that can trigger these acts of destruction. And the degree of exposure is an outcome of the fragmentation and specialization of our cities, the placelessness of our suburbs, and the lack of a shared social world with adults from whom children and youth could learn forms of appropriate conduct, including caring and tenderness, and where they could share celebrations and community events in an affirmation of human existence. "For their own good" they are isolated in special facilities or secluded in their own homes because the public world is considered too dangerous; and there they fall prey to a really dangerous world invisible to most adults.

Sissela Bok describes a television series, *Mighty Morphin Power Rangers* as "the most violent series of programs produced to date for young children... that may condition the youngest users to later enjoyment of sadistic interactive games. The Rangers have a wide range of gruesome methods for dispatching their foes: by pulverizing them, exploding them, strangling them, burning them, or zapping them... Such programs are popular even among two-to-three year olds", reports Sissela Bok. "They sit absorbed in front of their sets, drinking in the color, glamour, energy of these programs, then attempt to execute the strokes and kicks of the Rangers on their own, often continuing to do so at playgrounds and in schoolyards. The series is marketed to hundreds of millions of children the world over... (and) generates near hypnotic appeal for many. The shows are meant primarily as entertainment but they turn out to be learning experiences as well, providing role models and teaching attitudes, expressions, postures, bodily moves."[xvi]

Despite statements, reports and studies by the American Academy of Pediatrics[xvii], the American Psychological Association[xviii], child psychologists (Kagan, Aaron, Apfel Simon, Healy, etc.) the situation has worsened.

One reason is that digital technology does not lend itself to the representation of human encounters. Through coordinated finger movements it allows the child to explode and dismember and burn people. The "interactive" aspect of the information technology appears rather limited.

As we have suggested in our foreword, and in the book as a whole, society's political leaders, urban professionals responsible for the shape of our cities, and all of us – need to pay more attention to creating a real world, especially a public realm and urban public places where children and youth are together with adults in all aspects of their daily life, observe them at work, share in celebrations, informal or organized community events. Positive experience in a hospitable social world inoculates children against the attraction of violence.

Unless we shift attention to the real public world of human presences, unless we can recover hospitable physical and social environments, and be aware of the risks inherent in certain features of information technology, then the lives of some young people will be shaped by an alternative "virtual" world and its dysfunctional role models.

[i] Lewis Mumford once suggested that a third to one half of the land area of the Los Angeles basin is used for highways and parking.

[ii] According to interviews with the leading scientists involved in the development of the atom bomb, they had little awareness of the complex long range consequences (on human beings and the physical environment) of nuclear technology. See Robert Jungk, **Brighter than a Thousand Suns**.

[iii] The U.S. was spared this particular drug technology disaster through the efforts of an FDA official, Frances Kelsey, who was not convinced of the safety of the drug.

[iv] Recently the use of neuroleptic drugs for children and adolescents has come under question when it was learned that one of the young persons responsible for the Colorado school massacre was prescribed a drug with a potential unknown array of side effects.

[v] Neil Postman, **Technopoly**, New York, Alfred Knopf, 1992.

[vi] Amy Harmon, *"A Sad, Lonely World is Discovered in Cyberspace, Surprising Researchers"*, **New York Times**, August 30, 1998. p 1.

[vii] "Our new technologically enmeshed relationships oblige us to ask to what extent we ourselves have become cyborgs, transgressive mixtures of biology, technology, and code. The traditional distance between people and machines has become harder to maintain." From Sherry Turkle, **Life on the Screen**, Simon & Schuster, New York, London. 1995. p. 21.

[viii] Mark Slouka, **War of the Worlds**, New York, Basic Books, 1995.

[ix] Marshall McLuhan's assertion that "each new technology amputates the function it extends is still worth remembering!" See Marshall McLuhan, **Understanding Media. The Extensions of Man**, McGraw Hill New York. 1964.

[x] Perhaps the sheer technical skill of being able to communicate in cyberspace is itself a form of confirmation; but whether this is the same kind of experience as a pat, a friendly face, or a kind word is questionable.

[xi] Jane Jacobs, **Death and Life of Great American Cities**, New York, Random House, 1961.

[xii] American Psychological Association Commission on Youth and Violence, **Violence and Youth: Psychology's Response**, Washington DC, The American Psychological Association, 1993.

[xiii] Sissela Bok, **Mayhem. Violence as Public Entertainment**, Reading, MA, A Merloyd Lawrence Book, Perseus Books, 1998.

[xiv] John Naisbitt, **High Tech, High Touch**, New York, Broadway Books, 1999.

[xv] John Naisbitt, op. cit. p. 66

[xvi] Sissela Bok, op. cit. p. 78

[xvii] Committee on Communications, American Academy of Pediatrics, "Children, Adolescents and Television", **Pediatrics**, vol. 96, (October 1995), p. 786.

[xviii] American Psychological Association Commission on Youth and Violence, **Violence and Youth: Psychology's Response**, Washington DC, The American Psychological Association, 1993.

Appendix

A Brief Review of Reference Works

The following books were important influences on our work on the child and the city. A brief review will introduce them to the reader who may wish to read them at a future date.

Rene Dubos, **So Human An Animal**, Charles Scribner and Sons, New York, 1969.

Sometimes scientists, distinguished in their own field, address broader social issues. Like the physiologist Walter Cannon, who suggested in his book **The Wisdom of the Body** that concepts describing the functioning of the human organism are also relevant to social systems including cities, Rene Dubos, a renowned microbiologist, surveys much wider issues in his Pulitzer Prize winning book, **So Human An Animal**. Dubos draws parallels between the destruction of the natural ecology, and the fate of our urban environments.

Dubos believes that suburban environments have become inimical to the development of children and young people. "Children growing up in some of the most prosperous suburbs may suffer from being deprived of experiences." He contrasts their experience with that of children growing up in the streets of New York around in the 1900's which "despite its squalor and confusion proved one of the richest human environments that ever existed. Children there were constantly exposed in the street to an immense variety of stimuli."

Like Lewis Mumford, Jacques Ellul and other thoughtful scholars, Dubos raises questions about the uncritical adoption of every new technology that is promoted. He joins in the warning that to disregard the possible effects of technology "can amount to setting a time bomb that will explode in the face of society from a month to a generation in the future."

Andreas Feldtkeller, **Die Zweckentfremdete Stadt**, Campus Verlag, Frankfurt/New York, 1994.

This book is by the long time planning director of the city of Tübingen, responsible for the restoration of its inner city, who early on realized the importance of bringing children back to the city center. The book is a manifesto against the continuing destruction of public urban space, and a plea that the public realm is indispensable for meeting the historic social, cultural and educative mission of the city.

For Feldtkeller, children represent a seismograph for the tremors in the relations between city dwellers. The current fashionable promotion of the

A Brief Review of Reference Works   139

"Kinderfreundlichen Stadt" (child friendly city) implies the creation of a separate world for children (with their own play facilities, special "reservations" in parks, etc.) Such an approach, for Feldtkeller, represents the abandonment of the values that accrue when children and adults share the same social world.

Jane Jacobs, **Death and Life of Great American Cities**, New York, Random House, 1961.

Jane Jacobs' classic work, distinguished by its common sense, and unique among books on cities because it is based on first hand observations of every day urban life, may have had more impact on European city planners than on its original American audience. It is also unique among books on city planning in its concern with children in the city.

Whether she writes about lively sidewalks, city neighborhoods, or mixed use, she is always aware that children are part of city life, indeed they need the stimulation and the presence of adults for their play, socialization and social development.

The following observations by Jacobs illustrate why her book should be required reading for all responsible for the design of cities. Jane Jacobs on sidewalks: "Sidewalk width is invariably sacrificed for vehicular width because city sidewalks are conveniently considered to be purely space for pedestrian travel and access to buildings and go unrecognized and unrespected as the unique, vital and irreplaceable organs of city safety, public life and child rearing that they are."

And to city planners, and community activists who clamor for open space, she writes: "More open space for what? For mugging? For bleak vacuums between buildings? Or for ordinary people to use and enjoy? But people do not use open space just because it is there."

In talking with colleagues or reading well-intentioned reports by foundations, inevitably the majority intone the mantra for more playgrounds, youth facilities, "reservations" for children and youth. Jane Jacobs is clearly on the other side, where she is joined by more wholistic and more enlightened students of cities (such as Bernard Rudofsky, Colin Ward). Jacobs knows that "spaces and equipment do not rear children... but only people rear children and assimilate them into civilized society."

Suzanne H. Crowhurst Lennard and Henry L. Lennard, **Livable Cities Observed: A Source Book of Images and Ideas**, Gondolier Press, IMCL Council Publications, Carmel, 1995.

During the years of observations and analysis of cities summarized in **Livable Cities Observed** children received high priority. Indeed, this is one of the very few books in the area of planning or urban design that reflect a concern with children within the whole city's social and physical environment. Whether the subject is public space design, transportation policy, community festivals or public art, the effects on children's lives are of paramount concern.

It will be beneficial for the reader to become familiar with the broader survey of topics, issues and case studies provided in **Livable Cities Observed**. The ideas that formed the basis for **Livable Cities Observed** are further developed in this book.

Kevin Lynch, **Growing Up In Cities**, The MIT Press, Cambridge, MA, 1977.

Kevin Lynch's earlier, seminal work, **The Image of the City,** explains how we form an image of the city by identifying such physical elements as paths, edges, nodes, landmarks and districts. He proposes that "a distinctive and legible environment not only offers security but also heightens the potential depth and intensity of human experience... A highly imagable city would seem well formed, distinct, remarkable; it would invite the eye and the ear to greater attention and participation. The sensuous grasp upon such surroundings would not merely be simplified, but also extended and deepened."

While **The Image of the City** was addressed to city planners and urban designers, Lynch came to realize that the legibility and imagability of the city was of greatest relevance for children.

Growing Up In Cities edited by Kevin Lynch from reports by Tridib Banerjee and others, presents the images children have of their environment in diverse urban and suburban settings in Australia, Argentina, Poland and Mexico. The research emphasizes how important street environments are for children.

For example, those growing up in central city areas in Poland found their environment challenging and stimulating and produced elaborate, accurate maps of their area filled with detailed information. Children from the mass housing districts around the historic cities in Poland were hungry for the activity and stimulus they perceived was available in the city's center. In comparison, children growing up in suburban Melbourne were bored, uninterested and produced bare, repetitive maps of the area, lacking in detail.

These findings were intended to guide public policies for improving the urban and suburban environment for children.

Alice Miller, **Banished Knowledge**, Doubleday, New York 1990, and **Breaking Down the Wall of Silence**, Meridian, Penguin Books USA, New York 1993.

Alice Miller's work deserves serious attention from everyone concerned with the fate of children. Though it does not explicitly deal with the physical urban environment, her thesis, presented in a series of books from 1981 to 1993 is nonetheless important to our work.

Miller documents that children are mistreated and abused on a much larger scale than is admitted, that mistreatment and abuse results in much of the destructiveness, both on an individual and societal level, that concerns us today; and that, furthermore, the repression of one's own intolerable pain at such mistreatment becomes the basis for our subsequent failure to recognize, identify and empathize with the pain inflicted on children by parental lack of understanding, and by physical and emotional mistreatment.

"Parents who have never known love, who on coming into the world met with coldness, insensitivity, indifference and blindness and whose entire childhood and youth were spent in this atmosphere, are unable to bestow love... Nevertheless their children will survive. And like their parents they too will not remember the torments to which they were once exposed because those torments... have all been repressed, that is, completely banished from consciousness."

Miller's thesis has important implications for us: mistreatment of children leads to much of the destructive behavior that troubles our cities; but furthermore, adult inability to come to terms with childhood experiences provides the source for much of the distrust and suspicion prevalent among city dwellers.

Alice Miller's thesis of the repression of mistreatment inflicted on children may explain the failure to identify and empathize with children and their needs in the design of cities. Many adults do not remember, or wish to forget what it felt like to experience the social and physical world as a child. This failure to remember on the part of architects, planners, urban designers and city officials results in cities that are inhospitable and sometimes brutal environments for children. Indeed, some urban environments can be viewed as a form of child abuse.

Miller sees the attitudes and behavior of parents towards children as important for human development, as did Freud, but she goes beyond Freud in seeing child mistreatment as the single critical factor in the creation of violent criminals, including mass murderers such as Germany's Hitler and Romania's Ceaucesco.

Alexander Mitscherlich, **Die Unwirtlichkeit unserer Städte,** (**The Inhospitality of Our Cities**), Suhrkamp Verlag, Frankfurt, 1965; and **Thesen zur Stadt der Zukunft** (Theses for the City of the Future), Suhrkamp Verlag, Frankfurt ,1971.

These two paperback volumes, collections of essays, unfortunately not available in an English edition, have had considerable influence on the German dialogue about cities. What makes them unusual is that their author was Germany's best known psychoanalyst and pioneer in psychosomatic medicine.

It is hard to think of a mental health professional or intellectual of Mitscherlich's stature in the Anglo Saxon world who has similar interests and commitment to cities.

Mitscherlich shows how the forces shaping modern cities are making them inhospitable for most of their inhabitants, and especially for children and youth. He explains how this unsuitability of cities for the optimal emotional and social development of their inhabitants is responsible for an array of psychological problems, despair and aggressivity in cities.

Despite Mitscherlich's pessimism that his warning would not be heeded, the discussion that his books initiated may have prevented some of the worst features of North American cities to be transferred to Europe, especially to Germany. However, judging by current developments and discourse about cities in Germany, it seems that attention to his important insights has diminished.

Ray Oldenburg, **The Great and Good Place,** New York, Paragon House, 1991.

This interesting study by the sociologist Oldenburg concerns the loss of "third" places, public places where community members gather, that are easily accessible from where people live. Oldenburg's book, written without professional jargon, is a study of the decline of community in North American cities, town and suburbs, and the subsequent effect on the lives of children and youth. "The world of work excludes children for a great many Americans; the job offers a substitute community. But unlike the residential community of the past, it is one in which there is no place for children... Today's legacy to youth is one of isolation."

In contrast to other social scientists, Oldenburg does not believe that the shopping mall is an urban public place. "The shopping mall offers basic training in consumerism... it helps preserve the myth that America is a child-centered culture. That it's not much of a place in terms of excitement, interest or human development is easily overlook. Youngsters do not interact with adults at shopping centers."

Neil Postman, **The Disappearance of Childhood**, Vintage Books, New York, 1982, 1998; **Technopoly**, Knopf, New York, 1992; and an essay in **Notes of the Lead Pencil Club**, Pushcart Press, Wainscott, New York, 1997.

In the **Disappearance of Childhood**, Postman offers an intriguing and quite convincing thesis that the concept of childhood (the idea that children constitute a separate group of persons and deserve to be treated differently from adults) is a relatively recent phenomenon, now in decline. "The period between 1850 and 1950 represent the high watermark of childhood. In America successful attempts were made during these years to get all children into school and out of factories, into their own clothing, their own furniture, their own literature, their own games, their own social world."

Most important is Postman's claim that the mistreatment of children by parents, teachers and the society was in remission during those years. "As late as 1780, children (in England) could be convicted for any of the more than

200 crimes for which the penalty was hanging." During the middle 19th century, according to Postman (and the scholars he refers to), began "the period in which parents developed the psychic mechanisms that allow for a full measure of empathy, tenderness and responsibility toward their children."

For Postman, the modern electronic media usher in a childless world where children are exposed to the same communicational environment as everyone else. There is an increasing compassion deficit, and lack of identification with children. Even Postman may not have anticipated in 1983, when he wrote **The Disappearance of Childhood,** that a district attorney in California in 1997 would consider indicting a six year old boy for attempted murder.

More recently, Postman has continued his analysis of the effects of the electronic media, and the proliferation of computer use, with attention to how this technology has affected children. In **Technopoly,** Knopf, New York, 1992 and an essay in **Notes of the Lead Pencil Club,** Pushcart Press, Wainscott, New York, 1997, he is concerned with the Faustian bargain struck by the uncritical, wholesale adoption of this technology.

"The role that new technology should play in schools or anywhere else is something that needs to be discussed without the hyperactive fantasies of cheerleaders. In particular, the computer and its associated technologies are awesome additions to a culture... but like all important technologies of the past, they are Faustian bargains, giving and taking away, sometimes in equal measure, sometimes more in one way than the other. It is strange--indeed shocking--that with the twenty-first century so close, we can still talk of new technologies as if they were unmixed blessings--gifts, as it were, from the gods. Don't we all know what the combustion engine has done for us and against us? What television is doing for us and against us? At the very least, what we need to discuss... is what children will lose... if they enter a world in which computer technology is their chief source of motivation, authority, and, apparently, psychological sustenance."

Colin Ward, **The Child in the City**, The Architectural Press Ltd., London 1978

Colin Ward's generously illustrated landmark book about the fate of children in today's cities is even more relevant today than it was twenty years ago. The city, Ward says, "has failed its children. It fails to awaken their loyalty and pride. It fails to offer legitimate adventures." He decries the loss to the automobile of the city's streets as safe and interesting places to play; indeed, he believes that the whole city should be accessible to children.

Ward believes that play is a way to explore the world: children find inexhaustible fun discovering the possibilities of fire hydrants and fountains, steps and slopes, gratings and paving patterns, railings and sculptures to climb on. They learn from exposure to the rich resources of the city's life. He believes that to "grow into responsible adulthood" children must be given the opportunity to learn <u>about</u> the city, to <u>use</u> the city, to <u>control</u> the city, and to <u>change</u> the city.

"Modern urban life" Ward observes, "exposes the young to the cornucopia of consumer desires while progressively denying them the means of gratifying these expensive wants except through the munificence of parents." He believes that children in the city should have the chance to earn money and the opportunity to be useful.

He identifies two primary obstacles to acceptance of children in the city: the conception of the city as a mechanism for real estate profits; and the dominance of the automobile. "The theme that runs all through this book is that we have to explore every way of making the city more accessible, more negotiable and more useful to the child. We have seen that some children develop the habit of exploiting everything their environment can provide. They unfold as individuals through creatively manipulating their surroundings. But there are many others who never get a foot on that ladder, who are isolated and alienated from their city. Often they take revenge on it."

This book is as filled with observations, ideas and good references as a good city is filled with stimulating experiences and social encounters. It is an essential reference for all concerned with children in the city.

Acknowledgements

We have previously acknowledged the great debt that our work on cities owes to Lewis Mumford (The City in History), Bernard Rudofsky (Streets for People), G.E. Kidder Smith (Italy Builds), and Martin Buber (Ich und Du; Elemente des Zwischenmenschlichen). The influence of their ideas on this book, though it is not always self evident, is considerable.

We were also fortunate over the years to have engaged in dialogue about many of the issues we are wrestling with in this book with a number of colleagues and friends with very different professional backgrounds and perspectives. Among them we must mention Gregory Bateson, Ivan Boszormenyi-Nagy, Andreas Feldtkeller, Stephen Fleck, Peter Novak, Joseph P. Riley, Anselm Strauss, Wolf Von Eckardt, Sven von Ungern-Sternberg.

About the Authors:

Henry L. Lennard, Ph.D., Professor of Psychiatry and Sociology at the University of California Medical School, San Francisco. He founded the Family Study Station and the Center for the Study of Drugs and Social Behavior at the University of California Medical Center. He also held Professorships at the Pacific Medical Center, New York University, University of Colorado, University of Ulm, and other Universities in the US and Europe.

Dr. Lennard is the author of thirteen books, among them: *Anatomy of Psychotherapy; Patterns in Human Interaction; Mystification and Drug Misuse; Ethics in Health Care;* and *The Psychiatric Hospital;* co-author (with Suzanne Crowhurst Lennard) of *Public Life in Urban Places; Livable Cities, People and Places; Livable Cities Observed;* and co-editor of *Making Cities Livable.*

Professor Lennard's work on social behavior, families, children and drugs was supported by a Career Scientist Award from the National Institute of Mental Health, and by awards from the National Science Foundation, the Commonwealth Fund, the William T. Grant and Russell Sage Foundations.

Suzanne H. Crowhurst Lennard, Ph.D.(Arch.), Founder (1985) and Director of the **International Making Cities Livable Conferences;** Editor of the **Making Cities Livable Newsletter.** Dr. Crowhurst Lennard has held Professorships and other academic positions at the University of California, Berkeley; Oxford Polytechnic in Oxford; Harvard University; and the University of Ulm.

She was honored by awards from the National Endowment for the Arts, the Royal Institute of British Architects, and the Graham Foundation for Fine Arts.

Professor Crowhurst Lennard is author of *Explorations in the Meaning of Architecture* and the forthcoming *In Praise of Squares;* co-author of *Public Life in Urban Places; Livable Cities, People and Places;* and *Livable Cities Observed;* and co-editor of *Ethics of Health Care* and *Making Cities Livable.* Her publications have been acclaimed as important contributions to the understanding of cities by scholars and civic leaders from Lewis Mumford to Mayors Kronawitter (Munich) and Casellati (Venice); and by architectural critics G.E. Kidder Smith, Neil Pearce and Wolf Von Eckardt. Dr. Crowhurst Lennard is a Consultant on public space design in the US, Canada and Europe.

Bibliography

American Academy of Pediatrics, Committee on Communications. (1995) *"Children, Adolescents and Television"* in **Pediatrics**, Vol. 96, October.

American Psychological Association Commission on Youth & Violence. (1998), **Violence and Youth: Psychology's Response**, Washington DC, The American Psychological Association.

Donald Appleyard. (1981) *"The Street as a Place for Play and Learning"*, in **Livable Streets**, Berkeley, University of California Press.

Philippe Ariès. (1978) **Geschichte der Kindheit**, München, Deutsche Taschenbuch Verlag.

Walter Baruzzi. (1996) *"La Cittá in Tasca"*. Paper given at the 1996 **International Making Cities Livable Conference** in Venice.

Gregory Bateson. (1972), **Steps to an Ecology of Mind.** New York, Ballantine Books.

Sissela Bok. (1998), **Mayhem. Violence as Public Entertainment.** Reading, MA, Perseus Books.

Ivan Boszormenyi-Nagy.(1980) in **Ethics of Health Care,** Henry L. Lennard & Suzanne H. Crowhurst Lennard (Eds.). New York, Gondolier Press.

Martin Buber. (1954), *"Elemente des Zwischenmenschlichen"*, in **Die Schriften über das dialogische Prinzip**, Heidelberg.

-- (1957), *"Distance and Relation"* in **Psychiatry**, Vol. 20.

-- (1965) *"Dialogue"*, in **Between Man and Man**, MacMillian Publishing Co.

Walter Cannon. (1932), **The Wisdom of the Body.** New York, W.W. Norton Co. Inc.

Harvey Cox. (1969), **The Feast of Fools.** Cambridge, MA, Harvard University Press.

154 THE FORGOTTEN CHILD

Suzanne H. Crowhurst Lennard. (1978), *"The Child's Conception of Built Space"*, in **Education**, Winter 1978.

-- (1980) **Explorations in the Meaning of Architecture.** NY, Gondolier Press.

-- (1980), with Henry L. Lennard (Eds.). **Ethics in Health Care.** New York, Gondolier Press

-- (1983), *Architecture as Autobiography"* in **The Humanist,** Sept/Oct. 1983.

-- (1984), with Henry L. Lennard, **Public Life in Urban Places.** NY, Gondolier Press.

-- (1986) *"Physical Setting as Therapeutic Modality"* in **The Psychiatric Hospital,** New York, Human Sciences Press.

-- (1987) *"Towards Criteria for Public Art"*, in **Urban Land,** March 1987.

-- (1987), with Henry L. Lennard, **Livable Cities: Social and Design Principles for the Future of the City.** NY, Gondolier Press.

-- (1989) *"Making Cities Better for Children"* in **Urban Land,** June 1989.

-- (1993) *"Urban Space Design and Social Life"* in Ben Farmer & Hentie Louw (Editors), **Companion to Contemporary Architectural Thought,** London & New York, Routledge.

-- (1995) with Henry L. Lennard, **Livable Cities Observed: A Source Book of Images and Ideas** Carmel, CA, Gondolier Press.

-- (1997) with Sven Von Ungern-Sternberg, & Henry L. Lennard (Editors). **Making Cities Livable. Wege zur menschlichen Stadt.** Gondolier Press.

-- (2000) *"Why Cities Need Squares"*, in **Urban Land,** February 2000

-- (2000) *"Why Young People Need Squares"* in **Planning,** August, 2000.

Lloyd deMause. (1974) **The History of Childhood**, New York, The Psychohistory Press.

Rene Dubos. (1968) **So Human an Animal.** New York, Charles Scribner's Sons.

Leon Eisenberg. (1972) *"The Human Nature of Human Nature"*, in **Science,** April 1972.

Jacques Ellul. (1964), **The Technological Society,** Vintage Press.

Andreas Feldtkeller. (1994) **Die zweckentfremdete Stadt.** Frankfurt-New York. Campus Verlag.

Dietrich Garbrecht. (1981) **Gehen: Ein Plädoyer für das Leben in der Stadt,** Basel, Beltz Verlag.

-- (1993) *"Walkability: A Prerequisite for Livable Cities"* in Ben Farmer & Hentie Louw (Editors), **Companion to Contemporary Architectural Thought,** London & New York, Routledge.

Andreas Gestrich. (1992) *"Kinder in der Stadt"* in **Die Alte Stadt,** Frankfurt.

Ernst Gombrich. (1987) *"The Beauty of Old Towns"* in **Reflections on the History of Art.** Berkeley, CA, University of California Press.

Arno Gruen. (1997), *"Livable Cities. Children and their Needs"* in **Making Cities Livable. Wege zur menschlichen Stadt,** Suzanne H. Crowhurst Lennard, Sven Von Ungern-Sternberg & Henry L. Lennard, (Editors) Gondolier Press.

-- (1997), **Der Verlust des Mitgefühls,** München, Deutscher Taschenbuch Verlag.

Dietmar Hahlweg, (1997) Talk given at the **19th International Making Cities Livable Conference** on *Children and Youth in the City,* Charleston, SC, March 1997.

Amy Harmon. (1998) *"A Sad, Lonely World is Discovered in Cyberspace, Surprising Researchers",* **New York Times,** August 30, 1998.

Helmut Holzapfel. (1997) *"Autonomie statt Auto",* in **Economica,** Bonn.

Arianne Huffington. (2000) **How to Overthrow the Government.** Regan Books, Harper Collins.

Jane Jacobs. (1961), **The Death and Life of Great American Cities.** New York, Random House.

Jane Holtz Kay. (1998), **Asphalt Nation,** Crown Publishers.

Henry L. Lennard. (1969), **Patterns in Human Interaction,** San Francisco, Jossey-Bass Publishers. Reprinted 1970.

-- (1970) et al. *"Hazards Implicit in Prescribing Psychoactive Drugs"* in **Science,** 169. Reprinted in J.G. Burke (ed.) **The New Technology and Human Values,** Wadsworth Publ. Co.

-- (1971) et al. **Mystification and Drug Misuse: Hazards in Using Psychoactive Drugs,** San Francisco, Jossey-Bass Publishers. New York, Harper & Row Perennial Library Series, 1972.

-- (1972), *"Issues in Interaction Research"*, in **Family Interaction** (ed. By James Framo), New York, Springer Publishing Co.,

-- (1973) et al. *"The Cure Becomes a New Problem"*, in **Smithsonian,** 4.

-- (1974) *"Perspectives on the New Psychoactive Drug Technology"* in **Social Aspects of Psychoactive Drug Use** (ed. by R. Cooperstock), Toronto, Addiction Research Foundation.

-- (1980), with Suzanne H. Crowhurst Lennard (Eds.). **Ethics in Health Care.** New York, Gondolier Press.

-- (1980) *"Benzodiazepines, the Physician and the Disease Model"* in **Prescribing Practice and Drug Usage,** (ed. by R. Mapes), London, Croom Helm.

-- (1981) *"Role Strain and Tranquilizer Use"* in **Health and Canadian Society** (ed. by David Coburn, et al.) Pickering, Ontario, Fitzhenry and Whiteside Ltd..

-- (1984), with Suzanne H. Crowhurst Lennard **Public Life in Urban Places.** NY, Gondolier Press.

-- (1986) with Alexander Gralnick, **The Psychiatric Hospital,** New York, Human Sciences Press.

-- (1987), with Suzanne H. Crowhurst Lennard **Livable Cities: Social and Design Principles for the Future of the**

City. Southampton, NY, Gondolier Press.
-- (1988) *"The City for Children"* in **Making Cities Livable Newsletter**, Dec. 1988.
-- (1990) *"Towards Family Sensitive Health Care"* in **Primary Health Care** (P. Bergerhoff, P. Novak, et al, Ed), Berlin, Heidelberg, Springer Verlag.
-- (1990) *"Usable Public Spaces for Children and the Elderly"* in **Making Cities Livable Newsletter**, March/Sept. 1990.
-- (1995) with Suzanne H. Crowhurst Lennard **Livable Cities Observed: A Source Book of Images and Ideas** Carmel, CA, Gondolier Press.
-- (1997) with Suzanne H. Crowhurst Lennard, & Sven Von Ungern-Sternberg, (Editors) **Making Cities Livable. Wege zur menschlichen Stadt.** Gondolier Press.
Konrad Lorenz. (1986) **Der Abbau des Menschlichen,** München, R. Piper & Co. Verlag.
-- (1990), **On Life and Learning,** New York, St. Martin's Press.
Kevin Lynch. (1977) **Growing Up In Cities.** Cambridge, MA, The MIT Press.
Marshall McLuhan. (1964) **Understanding Media. The Extensions of Man.** New York, McGraw Hill.
Alice Miller. (1984) **For Your Own Good.** London, Virago Press.
-- (1990) **Banished Knowledge.** New York, Doubleday.
-- (1993) **Breaking Down the Wall of Silence.** New York, Meridian, Penguin Books USA.
Alexander Mitscherlich. (1968) *"Was soll aus unseren Städten werden?"* in **Bauen und Wohnen,** March 1968.
-- (1969) **Die Unwirtlichkeit unserer Städte.** Frankfurt am Main, Suhrkamp Verlag.
-- (1971) **Thesen zur Stadt der Zukunft.** Frankfurt, Suhrkamp Verlag.
Lewis Mumford. (1961), **The City in History.** New York, Harcourt, Brace & World, Inc.
-- (1963), **The Highway and the City,** New York, Harcourt, Brace & World, Inc.

John Naisbitt. (1999) **High Tech, High Touch**. New York, Broadway Books.

Ray Oldenburg. (1991) **The Great Good Place**. New York, Paragon House.

Constance Perrin. (1988) **Belonging in America**, University of Wisconsin Press.

Neil Postman. (1982) **The Disappearance of Childhood**. New York, Vintage Books, Reprinted 1988.

Neil Postman. (1992) **Technopoly**. New York, Alfred Knopf.

-- (1997) in **Notes of the Lead Pencil Club**. Wainscott, New York, Pushcart Press.

Bernard Rudofsky. (1969) **Streets for People**. New York, Doubleday & Company, Inc.

Wolfgang Schultz. (1994) *"Criteria for Urban Aesthetics"* in **Making Cities Livable Newsletter**, Vol. 4, No.1/2.

Vincent Scully. (1994) *"The Architecture of Community"* in Peter Katz, **The New Urbanism**, McGraw-Hill, Inc.

Mark Slouka. (1995) **War of the Worlds**, New York, Basic Books.

G.E. Kidder Smith. (1955), **Italy Builds**, New York, Reinhold Publishing Co.

Sherry Turkle. (1995) **Life on the Screen**, New York-London, Simon & Schuster.

US Department of Health & Human Services, National Center on Child Abuse & Neglect, (1996). **Child Abuse & Neglect: Case Level Data 1993**. Washington DC, US Government Printing Office.

Wolf Von Eckardt. (1982), **Live the Good Life**, New York, American Council for the Arts.

Colin Ward. (1978) **The Child in the City**. London, The Architectural Press, Ltd.

Index

DATE DUE

12-01-04			